WE HAVE THIS HOPE

VOLUME 1

We Have This Hope

HOPE

J.N. Andrews
A.G. Daniells
S.N. Haskell
Carlyle B. Haynes
Mrs. S.M.I. Henry
A.T. Jones
William Miller
Frank L. Peterson

W.W. Prescott
J.L. Shuler
Uriah Smith
W.A. Spicer
E.J. Waggoner
Ellen G. White
James White

VOLUME 1

TIMELESS ADVENTIST SERMONS

David C. Jarnes, compiler

Pacific Press® Publishing Association
Nampa, Idaho
Oshawa, Ontario, Canada
www.pacificpress.com

Cover design by Gerald Lee Monks
Cover design resources from Gerald Lee Monks
Inside design by Aaron Troia

Copyright © 2008 by Pacific Press® Publishing Association
Printed in the United States of America
All rights reserved

Unless otherwise indicated, all Scripture quotations are from the King James Version.
Scripture quotations marked ASV are from the American Standard Version, copyright © 1901.

Additional copies of this book are available by calling toll-free 1-800-765-6955 or by visiting http://
www.adventistbookcenter.com.

Library of Congress Cataloging-in-Publication Data
We have this hope : timeless Adventist sermons / John N. Andrews . . . [et al.] ; compiled and edited
by David C. Jarnes.
    p. cm. — (We have this hope; vol. 1)
    ISBN 13: 978-0-8163-2271-8 (hard cover)
    ISBN 10: 0-8163-2271-6
    1. Adventists—Sermons. 2. Sermons, American.
    BX6123.W4 2008
    252' .067—dc22
                                                    2008006039

08 09 10 11 12 • 5 4 3 2 1

Dedication

I dedicate this book to my father, Elder Haakon I. Jarnes,
and to my father-in-law, Elder Edwin C. Beck,
both of whom gave themselves to preaching the blessed hope,
and to my mother, Dorothy Emerson Jarnes,
and my mother-in-law, Jacquelyn Faucher Beck,
who preached by their lives and characters, if not from the pulpit.

Contents

———◆———

Contents

Preface

    This book comprises a collection of sermons: one by William Miller, the central figure of the movement from which the Seventh-day Adventist Church developed, and fourteen others by fourteen Adventist leaders, pastors, and evangelists of the nineteenth and early to middle twentieth centuries. These sermons cover a variety of subjects, from salvation and law-and-gospel to the second advent of Christ and the mission of the Adventist Church.

    The book doesn't present exact transcripts of the sermons—I have edited the sermons for ease of reading and, in many cases, for length. I have, however, attempted to preserve the character of the original presentation and to represent the speakers' thinking accurately. I may have put a word or two into the speakers' mouths for increased clarity, but I have tried to avoid putting thoughts into their sermons that weren't originally there.

    Most of these sermons have been published previously in other books or in magazines or other papers. In some cases that means they no longer contain the "appeal" with which the speakers originally concluded their sermons when they preached them.

    I obtained many of the sermons in this volume from the General Conference archives. I'm indebted to James R. Nix, director of the Ellen G. White Estate, and his book *Advent Preaching* for several of the other sermons that appear here, and to George Knight for his suggestions of sermons to consider including.

My prayer is that you, the reader, may find in the pages that follow deepened respect for the dedication of our spiritual forebears, renewed conviction regarding the truths they proclaimed, and increased inspiration to live for Christ as we await His return.

David C. Jarnes, compiler

CHAPTER 1

Dedicatory Sermon

J. N. Andrews

———————•◆•———————

John Nevins Andrews (1829–1883) served in many roles in the early years of the Adventist Church. His primary contribution, however, came through his work as a scholar and prolific author and editor. It was his study that convinced the denomination that the Sabbath should be observed from sundown Friday to sundown Saturday. He spent the last nine years of his life serving as the church's first denominationally supported foreign missionary. Andrews preached this sermon Sunday afternoon, April 24, 1879, at the dedication of the Dime Tabernacle, in Battle Creek, Michigan. As it appears here, the sermon has been edited extensively for length and clarity.

We have assembled today for the solemn act of dedicating this house as a place of worship for the Lord of hosts. It seems eminently proper that some statement should be made of the distinctive doctrines of the people who worship here and of the work that we are endeavoring to carry forward in this place and elsewhere.

I have chosen as the foundation of my remarks the portions of Scripture that have been placed upon the windows at the rear of this platform, for these are a distinctive enunciation of the principles that guide us and of the faith that we cherish. The scripture inscribed on the central window is, as some of you may be able to see, the Ten Commandments, or law of God. [The speaker read Exodus 20:3–17.] The scripture on the left-hand window reads: "Being justified freely by his grace through the redemption that is in Christ Jesus. Romans 3:24." And on the right-hand window: "Here are they that keep the commandments of God, and the faith of Jesus. Revelation 14:12."

The scriptures that I have chosen for the foundation of my remarks necessarily lead me to speak upon three important subjects. First, the views that we cherish with regard to the law of God; second, the views that we cherish with regard to the gospel of our Lord Jesus Christ; and, third, the views that we cherish with reference to our position in the fulfillment of prophecy.

First, then, I will call your attention to the views that we entertain concerning the law of God. I am sure that every right-minded person in this assembly must regard the relation that man sustains to the moral law of God as a question of immense importance and one that is worthy of the most serious attention and thought on the part of all intelligent men. We understand in common, I believe, with all who fear God that this law of God is the great rule of right. It is the embodiment of the principles of God's moral government. The nature of this law is such that the attributes of God forbid that it should ever be abolished. So long as the Almighty maintains the principles of right, so long must this sacred code remain in force.

We understand very well that distinct from this moral law there was another system of law, known as the ceremonial law, that was but a shadow of things to come, a representation in types and shadows of the good things promised in the gospel of Christ. This ceremonial law passed away when the great Sacrifice was offered for the sins of men. The law of which I speak, however, is the moral law of God, which contains the sum of man's duty toward God and toward his fellowman. The immutable principles of right that are here embodied represent to us the will of God concerning man and the distinction that God makes between right and wrong. In this respect I am happy to believe that there are none here this afternoon, or at least very few, who entertain any ideas different from our own, and that there is with us who are here entire unanimity in believing that this great rule of right, given by God for the purpose of governing mankind, is the standard by which all human actions should be tested.

The great rule of right

In the New Testament, certain declarations are made with regard to the moral law. The third chapter of 1 John states that sin is the transgression of the law, and in the third chapter of Romans and twentieth verse we have the declaration that by the law is the knowledge of sin. So we understand that the New Testament refers to the law of God as a great rule of right that shows what sin is and sets before us a perfect standard by which our conduct should be estimated. On this point I am happy to believe that there is on the part of those in this house entire agreement. But now I ask your pardon while I call attention directly to the fourth commandment as marking one of the important, distinctive features of the people who worship in this house and who have erected it for the purpose of advancing what they believe to be the cause of truth.

Now, let me say that although the denomination that we represent here today is young in years, the conclusion is not to be hastily formed that this people has advanced new doctrines. There are no new truths in the Bible. We do not come forward as the representatives of new principles and doctrines that we invite you to accept in place of the ancient truths of God's Word. Rather, we come before you as a people who are presenting certain ancient truths that have been lost sight of and trampled in the dust. Our mission work is like that of John the Baptist preceding the first advent of Christ, who called attention to the errors and wrongs that had arisen among the Jewish people and gave force to his testimony by saying, "Repent ye; for the kingdom of heaven is at hand."

This is precisely our work, to call attention to certain ancient truths— truths as ancient as the creation of our earth—and to endeavor by all means in our power to restore again to the proper observance of mankind these truths that have been trampled in the dust. When I read the fourth commandment, therefore, I call your attention to one of the grand points that we believe justify our existence as a distinct people and the work we have undertaken to do.

This fourth commandment does solemnly enjoin upon all who are amenable to it—and that is all mankind—the observance of that day upon which God rested from the work of Creation. This commandment does not justify the suggestion that we should render to God merely one-seventh of our time—that no particular day is set before us and we may choose any day we wish. The day upon which God placed His blessing is the day that is the subject of this commandment. I call your attention to a remarkable fact that stands in immediate association with the giving of the law of God—that about one month before the Ten Commandments were proclaimed upon Mount Sinai it pleased God to provide food for His people by sending manna from heaven. He did this in such a manner as to mark by three great miracles each week which day was the seventh day so that there was no possible chance for the children of Israel to doubt for a moment that a definite day was set for them.

I know well that it is now said that the resurrection of Christ has changed the Sabbath. But all intelligent Bible readers know that there is no such declaration as this to be found in the New Testament. There are no words spoken in the New Testament that furnish any evidence, except by inference of a very doubtful character, that the resurrection of Christ has any reference whatever to the fourth commandment. And you do well know that if we were to insert in the fourth commandment a reference to the resurrection of Christ, it would essentially change the language of the commandment. It is impossible to bring Christ's resurrection into the commandment.

We have no objection at all to people worshiping on the first day of the week. So far from this, it is with us a frequent custom to do this, as we have done this day. But we do object to them using those meetings as an excuse for neglecting to hallow the day set apart at the Creation of the world—for neglecting the day that God has commanded that we keep. It is all right to worship God on any day, but it is an imperative duty that the seventh day should be observed as a memorial of the Creation of the heavens and the earth.

Pardon me for another remark closely connected with this subject. In the New Testament there is a divine memorial of the resurrection of Christ, and it is not abstaining from labor on the first day of the week. Rather, the New Testament's memorial of the Resurrection is that when men repent of their sins and enter upon the service of Christ, they should signify this fact by being buried with Christ in baptism and raised from the water in His divine likeness. Every time the church celebrates this memorial of the resurrection of Christ, believers participate in it.

Here, then, are two ancient truths that have been lost sight of by a great number of our fellowmen. While they are not new truths, they are, nevertheless, truths that very many have trodden in the dust. Upon us as well as upon others rests the responsibility of attempting to raise them up before mankind. I say, therefore, that there is just reason on our part for attempting to hallow the rest day of the great Creator. Nay, more than this, there are just reasons why we should endeavor by all proper means to call the attention of our fellowmen to these great truths.

Justification by the law

Now, perhaps, people who are perfectly honest will suggest that we who keep the fourth commandment and all the other commandments are seeking justification by the law of God and are, therefore, fallen from grace. My response is this: a humble effort to keep God's commandments on the part of Christian men who are conscious that they have broken them is altogether another thing from seeking to be justified as though they were righteous and had never sinned against God. We hold, as expressed in the scripture on the left-hand window, that believers are "justified freely by his grace through the redemption that is in Christ Jesus" (Romans 3:24). Here, beloved friends, we are happy to unite with a great majority of those who are present on this occasion in the statement that we are justified from sin through the blood of our Lord Jesus Christ and that this is the sole ground of our justification before God.

What is it that condemns the sinner, and what holds him in condemnation? Only one answer can be given to these questions: the sinner is condemned because he has broken God's law. God never justifies the sinner until He has first caused that sinner to see his sins with such distinctness that he shall acknowledge his condemnation to be just.

Notice the important statement made by the apostle with regard to the ground of the justification and the manner in which it is accomplished. He states it thus: "Being justified freely by his grace." That is, being justified by God's free, unmerited favor extended toward us through the redemption that is in Christ Jesus. What are we to understand by this word *redemption*? It means the buying back of something that has been forfeited. In this sense the redemption of Christ Jesus is the act of our Lord Jesus Christ in offering His precious life in the place of the lives of all sinful men.

Why did the Lord Jesus Christ lay down His life for sinful men? Men had broken God's holy law and thus deserved to die. That law was so holy and that condemnation so just that there was but one way in which they could be pardoned and God still remain just—a great Substitute must be offered. Only one Being in the whole universe could make that sacrifice and become that Substitute. All other beings owed service, but the Son of God, who was One with the Father and existed with the Father before the creation of the angels, presented Himself as a sacrifice to the law of God. His life was accepted in place of the lives of those who had broken it.

My friends, this is the costly price of our redemption—the death of the Son of God. Let no one present here this afternoon suppose that it is a light thing to break God's law. Pardon could be extended to man only at an infinite cost on the part of Him who extends it to us. There are some conditions to this pardon: these are that men should repent of their sins and believe on the Lord Jesus Christ. You understand what repentance is—that men who have broken God's commandments should leave off breaking them. That repentance causes an entire change of conduct.

When men believe on the Lord Jesus Christ in order that they may be saved and find pardon for their sins, that faith is not a dead faith, not a mere assent to the doctrines of the New Testament. Rather, it is a living faith that produces obedience to God and leads men to keep His commandments. I understand the gospel of Christ to be the great remedial scheme by which men who have broken God's commandments shall be brought back again to the favor of God, their hearts changed by the grace of God, and their sins forgiven, and from that time forward they shall walk in obedience to the commandments of God until they shall walk through the gates into the city.

God has extended to us who are here a free and gracious offer of pardon. You have sinned against God, broken God's commandments, but there is a free offer of pardon; and I repeat to you that every man and woman who will return to God by repentance and faith, who will seek God and make an unconditional surrender to Him, will find pardon. I do most cordially invite all who have not done so, to make a sincere surrender to God here this afternoon and to find how gracious is the Savior to freely forgive their sins.

A solemn warning

My third point is introduced by the statement on the right-hand window—found in Revelation 14:12: "Here are they that keep the commandments of God, and the faith of Jesus." I call your attention to the fact that this is a part of the proclamation of warning found in the fourteenth chapter of Revelation. There, three great proclamations of warning are brought to view. The third is a solemn warning concerning the seven last plagues to come on the world at the close of its history. This warning closes with the statement I have just quoted. Following that statement, the sacred writer says that he looked, "and behold a white cloud, and upon the cloud one sat like unto the Son of man, having on his head a golden crown, and in his hand a sharp sickle"—representing the second advent of the Lord Jesus Christ or events immediately connected with it.

It is doubtless well-known to all who are here this afternoon that we are *Adventists*. That is to say, that we are believers in the grand event represented in the Scriptures as the descent of the Son of God from heaven in the clouds with power and great glory, accompanied by all

19

the hosts of heaven. Then, with the sound of a great trumpet, the just shall rise again to immortality and all the living shall be changed in a moment, in the twinkling of an eye.

We who have erected this house of worship believe that this event is near at hand. We are aware that this doctrine is unpopular; that it is often made the subject of ridicule on the part of those who have no faith in it. We are not able to see that there is any just ground for this. Many classes of people known as Adventists have set many times for this event. Perhaps this has given the public occasion to laugh at the prospect of the near advent of Christ. We have set no time for this event; we do not believe the precise time to be given in the Bible. But we do understand from the sacred Scriptures that this great event is impending and that the generation now on the earth will not pass away until this event takes place. We are therefore interested to call the attention of men to this prophecy that indicates the approach of the judgment. We want to call their attention to the work of preparation for these great events and that included in this preparation is the restoration of God's commandments, which have been trampled down. We call people to obedience to these commandments in the manner ordained in the Bible.

The popular view that the world will be converted before the coming of Christ is, in our estimation, a grand error, an error of modern origin—not an ancient faith of the church but a modern doctrine by which that ancient faith has been eclipsed. The period of a thousand years brought to view in the twentieth chapter of Revelation does not precede the coming of Christ but succeeds that event. It begins with the resurrection of the just and terminates with the resurrection of the wicked—and the resurrection of the just takes place at the coming of Christ.

To show that there is to be no such event as the conversion of the world, I have but to refer you to the parable of the wheat and tares. In Jesus' explanation of this parable, He said that the wheat and tares—which represent the righteous and the wicked—are to grow together until the harvest, which is the end of the world. Also, the twenty-fourth chapter of Matthew gives an outline of the gospel dispensation in which the sorrows and woes of the church are brought to view. This record terminates with the statement that the days preceding the coming of the Son of man will be like the days that preceded the Flood—days not of righteousness but of wickedness.

The book of Daniel contains four great lines of prophecy that lead us from the time of Nebuchadnezzar to the second advent of Christ. The prophecy given in the seventh chapter of Daniel can serve as a sample of these lines of prophecy. In Daniel 7 the prophet saw in vision four great beasts arise out of the sea. Upon the head of the fourth beast were ten horns, and among these ten horns a little horn came up, spoke great things against God, wore out the saints of the Most High, and thought to change times and laws. In the explanation it is said that these four great beasts are four empires that should bear rule over the earth. It is well-known what these were. Their names are given in other parts of the Bible. They were Babylon, Media-Persia, Greece, and Rome. The ten horns represented the ten kingdoms into which Rome was to be divided. This division took place four hundred years after Christ.

The little horn that thought to change times and laws represents, beyond all dispute, that priest-king—the papal power—that arose in Europe immediately after the division of the Roman Empire and that has accomplished this very work against God's people and the law of God. The space of its dominion is given as a time, times, and a half, and this is explained to be 1,260 days. These days, in turn, are explained in the fourth chapter of Ezekiel to represent years, a day for a year. Beginning with the time the papal Roman kingdom came into power in A.D. 538, this period brings us down to 1798, when the dominion of the papacy was taken away. Eventually, it is to be consumed and destroyed, and then the judgment sits. Every feature of this prophecy has been accomplished, and now the great day of judgment is an impending event.

The last generation

I refer you also to the twenty-fourth chapter of Matthew. This chapter gives an outline of events during the gospel dispensation, showing the calamities, plagues, persecutions, and distresses that should come on God's people. It brings us down through the Dark Ages to the close of that persecution. The sun was to be darkened, which took place in 1780; and the moon was to be darkened too, which took place in 1833. This carries us to the generation that Christ said should not pass away until these things be fulfilled.

I would be glad to trace these lines of prophecy through Revelation also, but time will not permit me to do it. Suffice it to say that we are brought down to what we believe to be the last generation—the one to whom the third angel's message is directed. We are the people living in the age addressed by these warnings.

The closing part of this great warning says, first of all, that it relates to the great time of trouble that will come upon the world before the deliverance of God's people, when the seven last plagues shall be poured out upon all mankind. No other words have such awful solemnity as do these. None are so calculated to incite us to repentance, self-denial, cross-bearing, and patience.

The statement on the window from the twelfth verse of Revelation 14 is connected with this solemn admonition of God that the time of trouble is before us. The third angel concluded, "Here is the patience of the saints: here are they that keep the commandments of God, and the faith of Jesus." We understand the commandments referred to here to mean the Ten Commandments spoken by God—those that constitute the moral law and that stand distinct from the gospel of Jesus Christ. By the "faith of Jesus" we understand the teachings of the Savior as given in the New Testament. "Here are they that keep" not one, but all of the commandments of God and the faith of our Lord Jesus Christ. These two statements, so far from conflicting with each other, are in perfect harmony. The gospel of Jesus Christ shows how men who have broken the commandments of God may be pardoned and God yet maintain His justice.

"Here are they," says the prophecy, and we believe it to relate to our time, and even to the humble people who are engaged in this work. The people of God at that particular time are keeping His commandments. They are keeping them all. To break the commandments, it is necessary to break only one. Saint James's rule on this is very stringent: "Whosoever shall keep the whole law, and yet offend in one point, he is guilty of all. For he that said, Do not commit adultery, said also, Do not kill. Now if thou commit no adultery, yet if thou kill, thou art become a transgressor of the law" (James 2:10, 11).

So the apostle lays it down as a rule that if we break one of God's commandments, we become guilty of breaking the whole law of God. Thus when it is said in the fourteenth chapter of Revelation, "Here are they that keep the commandments of God," it does not announce a people that keep nine of God's commandments, but a people who keep all of them.

So I will leave this thought with you this afternoon: this house has been erected by a people who believe that the commandments of God are all sacredly binding and that they are not changed by the gospel of our Lord Jesus Christ. We believe that the period through which God's commandments have been trampled under foot is marked in prophecy and that we have come to the time when their restoration is to take place. We believe that work is entrusted to a people now on earth, and we ask all who are here present to participate in this sacred work.

This house has been erected in the hope that it will be the means of turning many to the testimonies of God and leading them to pay attention to the grand event that we believe is impending—the judgment and the coming of our Lord Jesus Christ. Therefore, we extend to our friends here present this afternoon the most cordial invitation that they meet with us from time to time to listen to these great themes and judge from these weighty truths if the judgment is at hand and if there is need of that preparation which will make us ready for that great event. May God add His blessing to these feeble remarks, through Jesus Christ our Lord. Amen.

CHAPTER 2

Christ's Power to Save

A. G. Daniells

———————◆◆◆———————

Arthur Grosvenor Daniells *(1858–1935) was a pioneer Adventist missionary to New Zealand and Australia, becoming closely associated with Ellen G. White during the time she spent Down Under. He was elected president of the General Conference in 1901 and continued in that position till 1922, handling well the many theological, administrative, and personnel difficulties that the church faced during his administration. He was particularly concerned with the development of spirituality in the church's ministers. Daniells preached this sermon Friday night, May 28, 1926, at the General Conference Session in Milwaukee, Wisconsin.*

I will greatly rejoice in Jehovah, my soul shall be joyful in my God; for he hath clothed me with the garments of salvation, he hath covered me with the robe of righteousness, as a bridegroom decketh himself with a garland, and as a bride adorneth herself with her jewels. For as the earth bringeth forth its bud, and as the garden causeth the things that are sown in it to spring forth; so the Lord Jehovah will cause righteousness and praise to spring forth before all the nations. For Zion's sake will I not hold my peace, and for Jerusalem's sake I will not rest, until her righteousness go forth as brightness, and her salvation as a lamp that burneth. . . .

I have set watchmen upon thy walls, O Jerusalem; they shall never hold their peace day nor night: ye that are Jehovah's remembrancers, take ye no rest, and give him no rest, till he establish, and till he make Jerusalem a praise in the earth (Isaiah 61:10–62:1, 6, 7, ASV).

It is quite plain from these scriptures that two important features are set before us. First is the glorious high purpose of God regarding sin and the redemption of men from it. Second is the cooperation that He expects from those who desire this redemption. Both phases of this great redemptive work are important. They are vital. In the first place, we have God's determination set forth—not only His desire, but His purpose, for He says, "as the earth bringeth forth its bud, and as the garden causeth the things that are sown in it to spring forth; so the Lord Jehovah will cause righteousness and praise to spring forth before all the nations."

In this dark world of sin, among the peoples that are war-mad, sin-polluted, full of idolatry and wickedness, and rebellious against God, He purposes to cause His righteousness to be revealed, to spring forth. And in the manifestation and revelation of His glorious character among all the nations of the earth there will be men and women who will say, "I will greatly rejoice in Jehovah, my soul shall be joyful in my God; for he hath clothed me with the garments of salvation, he hath covered me with the robe of righteousness, as a bridegroom decketh himself with a garland, and as a bride adorneth herself with her jewels."

But God calls for the cooperation of the church in the revelation of His righteousness before all nations. He doesn't plan that His people shall sit with folded hands, expecting Him to do this of Himself. O that we here tonight may respond to this gracious invitation of God! It is the only way we can share in the working out of this great plan of redemption from sin. It is our privilege to enter into this great work of God that He has set forth here, to cause His righteousness to be revealed. That righteousness is to be revealed through His people, through His church, and when we seek Him with all the heart, He will be found. When we loathe sin and confess it to Him, He will forgive our sins; He will cleanse us from all unrighteousness and heal us and redeem us.

Three angels' messages

There is another scripture I wish to read at this point in connection with this study. You are quite familiar with it. It is in the fourteenth chapter of Revelation. [The speaker read Revelation 14:6–14, the three angels' messages.] The purpose of God is expressed in this scripture: "Here is the patience of the saints: here are they that keep the commandments of God, and the faith of Jesus."

Where are these triumphant people found? Just where God's people are commissioned to proclaim the message that is to bring out such a people, and that is in every nation, every kindred, every tongue, every people on the face of the earth. That is where they are found. And what is said of them? They keep the commandments of God and the faith of Jesus. Man can never attain to anything greater than that. The commandments of God express His righteous character; they are an expression of His righteousness. There is no possible way by which any human being ever can keep those commandments except by the faith of Jesus.

And there is no greater faith, there is no other faith, no purer faith, than the faith of Jesus.

So these people, I take it, reach the highest point of excellence. They come to the highest platform of experience that the church has ever reached—that man will ever be required to reach. There is nothing higher. And throughout the wide world, in all nations, God will have a people keeping His commandments of righteousness through faith in His own dear Son.

Here is the cooperation of the church: "I saw another angel fly in the midst of heaven, having the everlasting gospel to preach unto them that dwell on the earth." None of us understand that these angels are doing this work independently of the church. We know full well that this scripture embraces the church, the people of God—those who have heard the commandments, those who have learned of the faith of Jesus, those who have been led to take their stand for it and who go forth to every nation, kindred, tongue, and people, to proclaim this great three-fold message of God to the world. As they go forth telling this message in all lands, to all peoples, under all conditions, the blessing of God attends them, and others are led to take their stand for this message. As they endeavor to render obedience to it, God blesses them and brings them onto this high platform of Christian experience.

We see a marvelous exhibition of the working out of this glorious plan of God as set forth in the scripture I have read, for here tonight we have men and women gathered from all parts of the world, from many nations, from places where people are in the darkest idolatry there is in the world. They are here to testify that God has so blessed the giving of this message that they in their heathen darkness have been delivered, have been set free. They have been given help and power from God, and He has lifted them to the high place of keeping the commandments of God through faith in His dear Son. It is being accomplished.

So here we see God's great purpose, and we see cooperation with God on the part of His people, the church. Dear friends, it works marvelously.

Here is another passage: "I saw, and behold, the Lamb standing on the mount Zion, and with him a hundred and forty and four thousand, having his name, and the name of his Father, written on their foreheads." "These are they that were not defiled with women; for they are virgins. These are they that follow the Lamb whithersoever he goeth.

These were purchased from among men, to be the firstfruits unto God and unto the Lamb. And in their mouth was found no lie: they are without blemish" (Revelation 14:1, 4, 5, ASV).

That is what it is to keep the commandments of God. It brings just such perfection of character.

And then in the book of Zephaniah, that little prophecy, we read, "The remnant of Israel shall not do iniquity, nor speak lies; neither shall a deceitful tongue be found in their mouth; for they shall feed and lie down, and none shall make them afraid" (Zephaniah 3:13, ASV).

"The remnant of Israel"—we know what that means: the last church, that church brought to view in the fourteenth chapter of Revelation, which will live to witness the appearing of our Lord and Savior in the clouds of heaven. His redeemed people. That people will be brought by the grace of God to this high Christian experience where they "shall not do iniquity, nor speak lies; neither shall a deceitful tongue be found in their mouth."

The apostle James tells us what it is to have complete victory over the tongue. He says that if we sin not in speech, if the tongue is sanctified and under complete control, the whole man is victorious. So we must conclude that the remnant will be brought to a state of Christian perfection as God intends. When God's great threefold message is carried to every nation, kindred, tongue, and people by His church, and when it lays hold of the hearts of men and women in all their varied conditions, in all those nations, and it brings them to this state, surely the righteousness of God will spring forth before all nations.

This is not mere theory, this great purpose of God and this cooperation of His people. This is being worked out; it is materializing right now. This fact should bring to us great encouragement, great assurance, and should lead us to that experience which is expressed in Isaiah, that we should never rest, never hold our peace, never cease our earnest cry to God until the righteousness of the Lord shines forth from His people to all the nations.

Divine experiments

I want to read a passage that I think is a revelation inspired to show us how fully this purpose of God is being wrought out in some measure for some connected with this great movement. In that little book *Testimonies to Ministers and Gospel Workers* I read this:

> The Lord Jesus is making experiments on human hearts through the exhibition of His mercy and abundant grace. He is effecting transformations so amazing that Satan, with all his triumphant boasting, with all his confederacy of evil united against God and the laws of His government, stands viewing them as a fortress impregnable to his sophistries and delusions. They are to him an incomprehensible mystery. The angels of God, seraphim and cherubim, the powers commissioned to cooperate with human agencies, look on with astonishment and joy, that fallen men, once children of wrath, are through the training of Christ developing characters after the divine similitude, to be sons and daughters of God, to act an important part in the occupations and pleasures of heaven.[1]

When the grace of God lays hold of people who have lived always in Satan's grip, when it delivers them, sets them free, and makes them children of Jesus Christ, Satan is amazed at the transformation. When he comes again to seek to exercise his control over them and finds them independent, finds them delivered, finds them free, finds his power broken, they are to him like an impregnable fortress. He can't get in, he can't manage them, he can't rule them as he once did. They are free, and as he looks on in his impotence, they are an amazing problem to him.

So God is working out His purpose. As the rain comes down and causes the earth to produce, the grass to spring up, and the leaves to put forth, so His Word, proclaimed by His servants, lays hold of hearts full of sin and causes sin to be washed away and the righteousness of Jesus Christ to be planted in its place. Oh, what a marvelous work God can do with humanity!

With regard to the cooperation God's people must exercise in this wonderful work, I read from *Testimonies to Ministers:*

> At this time the church is to put on her beautiful garments— "Christ our righteousness." There are clear, decided distinctions to be restored and exemplified to the world in holding aloft the commandments of God and the faith of Jesus. The beauty of holiness is to appear in its native luster in contrast with the de-

formity and darkness of the disloyal, those who have revolted from the law of God. . . . If, in defiance of God's arrangements, the world be allowed to influence our decisions or our actions, the purpose of God is defeated. . . . The church is firmly and decidedly to hold her principles before the whole heavenly universe and the kingdoms of the world; steadfast fidelity in maintaining the honor and sacredness of the law of God will attract the notice and admiration of even the world, and many will, by the good works which they shall behold, be led to glorify our Father in heaven.[2]

I have read considerable on this subject, for I desire tonight to help all to see that God is going to triumph in His purpose, notwithstanding all the opposition of the powers that are against Him. He will cause His righteousness to spring forth before all nations. He will redeem a people, but He will have the cooperation of His church. He will have us enter into that great undertaking with our whole hearts.

"Awake, awake"

Now I wish to read this statement in the fifty-second chapter of the book of Isaiah: "Awake, awake, put on thy strength, O Zion; put on thy beautiful garments, O Jerusalem, the holy city: for henceforth there shall no more come into thee the uncircumcised and the unclean. Shake thyself from the dust; arise, sit on thy throne, O Jerusalem: loose thyself from the bonds of thy neck, O captive daughter of Zion" (ASV).

Here we have surely a most earnest and powerful exhortation to enter into this great work and purpose of God. First He gives us an awakening call: "Awake, awake!" That call implies a measure of sleepiness. God wouldn't call us to awake if we were not in some measure sleepy.

Then God says, "Put on thy beautiful garments, O Jerusalem." We know this beautiful garment is the robe of Christ's own righteousness. And here we have a most earnest appeal to turn our hearts toward God and seek for His righteousness for the purity of heart that He designs all shall have whom He will translate to His kingdom above.

He says, "Put on thy strength, O Zion." We read that Christ is the power of God, and He declares that all power in heaven and in earth has been given to Him. And He tells His church to seek for that power, to seek for it before they can hope to have much success in proclaiming His message. He said to His disciples, "Ye shall be baptized in the Holy Spirit not many days hence," and "ye shall receive power, when the Holy Spirit is come upon you" (Acts 1:5, 8). This is the strength, the power, that He exhorts us to seek with all our hearts.

Then He says, "Shake thyself from the dust." I take it that dust represents sin in all its forms. "Shake thyself from the dust; . . . loose thyself from the bonds of thy neck, O captive daughter of Zion."

It seems to me, dear friends, that this is a most beautiful and encouraging message to come from God to us here tonight. As we enter upon this conference session, I believe that it would now be pleasing to God for us to listen to this appeal, to this counsel and instruction that He gives us, to turn away from sin, to seek for greater purity of heart, to seek for His righteousness. Then, as we return to our fields in all lands, we may go revealing the glories and the beauties of the righteousness of our Lord and Savior Jesus Christ!

In this connection I want to read another beautiful passage that I find here in the book *Christ's Object Lessons,* page 163:

> As the sinner, drawn by the power of Christ, approaches the uplifted cross, and prostrates himself before it, there is a new creation. A new heart is given him. He becomes a new creature in Christ Jesus. Holiness finds that it has nothing more to require. God Himself is "the justifier of him which believeth in Jesus." . . . And "whom He justified, them He also glorified." . . . Great as is the shame and degradation through sin, even greater will be the honor and exaltation through redeeming love. To human beings striving for conformity to the divine image there is imparted an outlay of heaven's treasure, an excellency of power, that will place them higher than even the angels who have never fallen.[3]

What a mighty incentive we have for this gospel work we are endeavoring to carry forward! As we go unto the nations about us, as we go out into the streets where sin seems to triumph, it is our privilege to know that God is at work for the sincere and for those who may be longing for deliverance—and thousands and thousands of people are.

It is our privilege to know that God sees them, that He knows the breathings of their hearts, and that He has the power to set them free—the power to deliver them, to impart to them His own righteousness, and to fit them to live in His presence with angels, with unfallen beings, and to enjoy that world forever and ever.

It is a great opportunity we have before us. Tonight may the Lord Himself inspire us with a burning desire to cooperate with Him in carrying out His high and glorious purpose for the redemption of this lost world.

Now, let us read again this beautiful statement that we started with, "I will greatly rejoice in Jehovah." As I read that yesterday morning at an early hour, my heart was lifted up to pray to God to put that joy and rejoicing into my heart. We labor, we toil, we sacrifice, but may we rejoice in it all. May we have the joy that God wants to have accompany all this labor and sacrifice and effort for Him. "I will greatly rejoice in Jehovah, my soul shall be joyful in my God; for he hath clothed me with the garments of salvation, he hath covered me with the robe of righteousness, as a bridegroom decketh himself with a garland, and as a bride adorneth herself with her jewels" (ASV).

It is a very vital experience for every minister and gospel worker to know for himself that his sins are surely and truly forgiven, that they are washed away, that he is cleansed from all unrighteousness, and that God has clothed him with His own righteousness. If we enter into that experience personally, it will have the greatest power and give us the greatest assurance and the greatest success of anything I know of in carrying God's message to the world.

Charley's testimony

Some little time ago I was going down the street of a Western city when a gospel wagon drew up to a corner and a man arose and began to talk about Jesus Christ to those who were standing on the corner. After telling us that Christ is a complete Savior, that He has all power, that He can lay hold of the most sinful man in the world and deliver him and make him righteous and pure and good, he said to us, "How do I know? My dear friends, I know He can do this because He has done it for me." And he looked earnest and confident as he said,

Do you want to know how I know He has done it for me? Well, I will tell you. Once I was a poor drunkard. I was brought up to use intoxicating liquors from a boy, and liquor became my master, and I became degraded, dishonored my father and my family, got into great trouble, and fled from my country. I went out to Australia, a new land to me, where I thought I could start all over and live a decent life. But when I got there I found my old appetite with me, and I found the land full of liquor, and I found sin on every hand. My environment was no better than that where I had lived, and so I was in sin and couldn't help it. I got into great trouble there, was imprisoned, and finally, when released, thought I would go over to America—God's country, as they called it.

When I landed there in Seattle, I found just what I had left in my native land—myself and all the sin about me, and soon I was in great trouble again. I was imprisoned, a long imprisonment, a heavy ball was chained to my ankle, and there I was in that desperate state.

One day a good, earnest preacher of the gospel came to the prison, and he talked very earnestly to us men. He told us that Christ was able to save us from all these conditions in which we found ourselves. I longed for such a deliverance. When he had finished, I went to my cell and fell down on my knees and cried to God, and I said, "O Lord, I don't know You. I don't know how to pray. I don't know Jesus. But Your man told me about You, and now if You can save a man from sin, O Lord, take hold of me and deliver me." I cried most earnestly and sincerely from the depths of my heart, and my friends, something came into my heart that I had never known before. There was power in it, and it made me hate sin and begin to love that which was good. I gave up my tobacco. I gave up liquor and profanity and vulgarity. I loved to read the Bible. This work went on until I was entirely transformed.

After a while I was paroled, and I went to work. When I found I was an entirely free man, delivered from all those habits, I wrote to my wife in the country where I had left her and told her that Charley was another man now, and I asked her if she would not come to me. She wrote back and said, "Charley, I don't know that what you have written is true, and I can't come until I know it. Can you get some one to testify for you?"

Charley said he went to the mayor and to other men in high positions there in the city and told them his story, and they wrote some beautiful testimonials for him, which he sent to her. He said so much time had passed that he had got a little home at the corner of a street. Finally his wife said, "Charley, I am coming." He said, "I met her and took her down to the little home that I had prepared, and we lived a happy, sweet, beautiful life from the day she arrived. And now, my friends, if you want to know whether all this is true, just come down there to that street and ask my wife."

When he got through, I think about all the men standing around there were wiping their eyes. I know I was. The power of his personal testimony as to what God had done for him laid hold of our hearts. That is what I have set forth here. May God help us to know the power of a redeemed life and of victory over sin—the power to be patient, to be kind, to be forbearing, to be victorious over the faults that we have and these evil dispositions of ours. Brethren, let us do just what is set forth here: "For Zion's sake will I not hold my peace, and for Jerusalem's sake I will not rest, until her righteousness go forth as brightness, and her salvation as a lamp that burneth."

I take that to mean that I, that you, that we as individuals here, ought to set our hearts most earnestly and determinedly to reach this victory brought out here—that we should cry to God until we know that our hearts have been redeemed, that His righteousness clothes us, and that it shines forth from us. If everyone attending this General Conference can enter into this blessed experience more fully than we ever have and go back to all our places of residence and fields of labor clothed with this beautiful garment of Jesus—this robe of righteousness—and live unsullied lives in labor for others, in compassion and self-sacrifice and devotion to Him, and live for those around us for whom we are to work, O, how His righteousness will spring forth before all nations and bring glory to His name!

1. Ellen G. White, *Testimonies to Ministers and Gospel Workers* (Mountain View, Calif.: Pacific Press®, 1923), 18.

2. Ibid., 16, 17.

3. Ellen G. White, *Christ's Object Lessons* (Mountain View, Calif.: Pacific Press®, 1900), 163.

CHAPTER 3

The Study of the Bible

S. N. Haskell

Stephen Nelson Haskell (1833–1922) was ordained as a Seventh-day Adventist minister in 1870. He served as a conference president, led the group that opened missionary work in Australia and New Zealand, taught Bible at Avondale College, held Bible training schools and evangelistic meetings, and authored several books. He gave this Bible study Friday morning, February 3, 1893, in Battle Creek, Michigan. It was the seventh in a series on the study of the Bible that he presented to the ministerial institute that preceded the General Conference Session.

Two thoughts very forcibly impress my mind this morning.* One is that we experience salvation just in proportion as we believe and weave into our character the testimony of God. We get no more than that, and it is on that scale that we shall be judged on the day of judgment.

The other thought is that we must believe that the Word of God is addressed to us, that it is a preserver to keep us from sin and a restorer to bring us back to what we would have been had we not sinned. However, not only must we believe that, but we must also believe that the Word is a creator. We must believe that it creates in our hearts the principles it teaches and that it does so as we study it. When we see that our lives are not in strict conformity to its principles, we take that Word as creating in our hearts those principles. If we do not take it as having this creating power, we shall not be saved. I don't believe we can ever appreciate the testimonies that we have from the Spirit of Prophecy, showing how God looks upon us, and how we should study the Scriptures, until we take them [the Scriptures] as containing the power of God to create.

We see this in David's experience. One night he had come upon Saul sleeping and had taken his cruse of water and his spear but had spared his life. Then he had called out to him from a distance to show him that he had had him in his power and had not slain him. He said, "Behold, as thy life was much set by this day in mine eyes, so let my life be much set by in the eyes of the LORD, and let him deliver me out of all tribulation. Then Saul said to David, Blessed be thou, my son David: thou shalt both do great things, and also shalt still prevail. So

---

* Just before Elder Haskell addressed the audience, Elder O. A. Olsen, General Conference president, read aloud a testimony from Mrs. Ellen G. White appealing to those present to set about the work of cleansing and purification.

David went on his way, and Saul returned to his place" (1 Samuel 26:24, 25).

Years before, God had told David that he was king of Israel. He had been anointed king, and he believed he was the rightful king. Now the Lord brought him into a place where he could fight his own battles or implicitly trust in the Lord to fight them for him. If the God who had anointed David to be king was going to place him upon the throne, what was it David's business to do? To trust God. But now there arose a counterinfluence that meant to defeat the purposes of God and keep David from the throne. What was David to do in that case? Was he to fight it out? No, he just simply trusted God. He allowed that principle to be worked into his character. He believed so firmly what God said that it regulated all his life. And now he asks the Lord to deal with him according to the way that he—David—had dealt with Saul. The prayer based upon such a foundation as that will always be heard.

No matter what the circumstances may be, God will let His principles manifest themselves in the heart that is yielded to Him. The man who lifts his hand against the soul thus trusting in God is lifting his hand against our Lord Jesus Christ. The Lord throws over that soul His righteousness and His covering, and God will carry that soul safely through.

I thought of this when that testimony was read this morning. Who does that apply to? It applies to me, and I thank God it applies to me. As Brother Jones says, if the reproof applies to me, that precious promise does also. But if I am so shrouded in self-righteousness that the reproof didn't hit me, where is the promise? I pity the man who has so much self-righteousness that he cannot take reproof from the Almighty. It is up to us to go down to the very bottom of the matter and find whether or not we believe in God. It is high time to find out whether God is talking to us or whether it is merely words, simply a form.

Well, says one, there seems to be so much of the human in the message.

This attitude is what led the Jews to perdition, and on this same ground many will go down to hell. They can see the human but not the divine.

Can you comprehend Christ? Did He not come in humanity? Now, just separate the humanity from the divinity if you can. The Jews saw the human all the time, but they didn't see the divine. Judas took in the divine as a general fact just as many Seventh-day Adventists take in the truth of God. Judas was anxious to be Christ's disciple, and the Savior took him. But Judas knew not the divine nature of the Son of God. He never believed that the word of Christ had the power to create and change the soul.

This is where our salvation lies—it rests upon the belief that the testimony of God contains the creative power to change our hearts and make us like Christ. Judas was ordained and commissioned to go out and labor. He was given the same opportunity to develop and to take hold of the power of God that Peter and the other disciples had. But he didn't weave these principles into his soul, and he reached the point where he was willing to sell his Lord for thirty pieces of silver just as a man would sell a horse or a cow. His own impulses and passion gained the mastery.

Every one of us has the divine in us, more or less, because every ray of light comes from Jesus Christ. Every man who ever walked the earth has had more or less of that divine life in his heart, and if any man will take it and treasure it, he will come to Christ. He is "the true Light, which lighteth every man that cometh into the world." I don't care if a heathen never heard of Jesus Christ; if he has had the conviction of right and wrong, it came to him from Christ. If he took it and treasured it, it would be, indeed, the saving knowledge of Christ, and he would be led into greater light.

There is something in Christ that can save us, every one of us in this house, and do it now, and give us a full and free salvation if we will only take His testimony and believe it as the power to change the character. My only hope lies in this. I know I have temptation and passion and humanity about me just as well as other people know it. Can I overcome them? Never. I want a strength or power that will put love where hate is and make me different—that will take all the mainspring of my affections and change them all over. O brethren, let us have the creating power of God!

I want to read some texts to prove that is just what God means, that there is a creative power in this work to affect hearts. John 6:63 says, "It is the Spirit that quickeneth; the flesh profiteth nothing: the words that I speak unto you, they are spirit, and they are life." The Spirit and the Word are both the same thing.

If it is in the Word and the Word quickeneth, why does it not quicken me?

If it does not, it is because I don't believe it. If I would take it in the proper light, would it not do it? The Word comes to me just as I take it.

Read a little farther and you will see that Judas never saw the creating power of God. Verses 64 and 65 say, "But there are some of you that believe not. For Jesus knew from the beginning who they were that believed not, and who should betray him. And he said, Therefore said I unto you, that no man can come unto me, except it were given unto him of my Father."

Those who "believed not" didn't believe in the sense that Jesus spoke of in the sixty-third verse. In one sense there was a belief, and in another sense there wasn't. Unless we cultivate the rays of light that shine into the soul during this conference, there is great danger of it becoming so common that it will lead us to sell our Lord just as practically as Judas did, and we will be left to perish.

We will read a number of other scriptures where the word *quicken* appears. John 5:21 says, "As the Father raiseth up the dead, and quickeneth them; even so the Son quickeneth whom he will."

He raises the dead. The body is dead—dead just like the earth. What does He do? He "quickeneth" it. Then is it not a creative power that comes into that body? What does the quickening? It is His word. God speaks and there is creation, there is a coming into existence, a life that was not in that clay before.

Then if I die believing in Christ, do you think I will come up again?

Oh, yes.

I would like to know on what authority I will come up.

On that of the Word of God.

Suppose I am troubled with some evil passions, that I am a covetous man. I have a big farm and will not sell it, for it seems too big a sacrifice. I read the Bible and find promises that show that by repentance I can become strong and that desire will go from me.

How can I get it out of myself?

I will just believe God.

Will it go out of me then?

Yes. The great trouble with many is that they never believe it. They go along always wrestling with their evil passions, and at the day of judgment they will be trying and will go to destruction trying at the last.

Then what shall we do?

Believe there is creative power in God's Word and take it out for yourself.

How can you believe it?

Educate your mind to believe it. Take God at His word.

Where the Amazon River flows into the sea, it carries fresh water many miles out into the sea. I remember reading about a shipwrecked crew who were floating off the mouth of the river. When they sighted a vessel at last, they signaled that they were perishing for water. The other ship flashed the signal back, "Dip."

But they said, "We cannot drink salt water," so again they signaled that they wanted water.

Again the signal came to dip.

Then the captain said, "They say, 'Dip,' so let us dip," and they dipped into the water that was all around them and found it fresh.

I tell you, we have an Amazon all around us and the signal from heaven is "Dip." And I say in the name of the Lord, let us dip! If you have the old passion and Satan has a mortgage on your body, let us discharge that mortgage by our Lord Jesus Christ. I am glad there is creative power in the Word of God. There is not only power to sustain but there is also something there to create, to make me a different man. That is all I hope in.

Romans 4:17 says that Abraham believed "God, who quickeneth the dead, and calleth those things which be not as though they were." Do you believe Abraham got salvation when he believed the things that were not as though they were? Is not that the very time that God said, "Abraham believed God, and it was accounted to him for righteousness"?

What did Abraham believe? The Word of God. In the natural course of events there was no probability or possibility of his being the father of many nations and the earth being blessed through him. But Abraham believed God; and the first line that you believe of God's Word on His authority, He will make it so to you.

You may say that Abraham proved untrue afterwards, but that was where Abraham tried to mix in some of his own works. Abraham thought he would do something himself. But the Lord never accepted Abraham's works. He brought him back over the same old road and made him believe that He meant just what He said. And when we come to believe that God means just what He says, there is salvation in it every time.

You can never train your mind to believe until you take the Bible and read it as though God was talking to your soul. If I read the Bible in the third person, it will do me no good. If I say that Paul was writing to the Romans, then it doesn't mean me; and if it doesn't mean me, there is no salvation in it for me. But I think it means me, and I am glad there is a power that can be transferred from God's Word to my soul. That Word becomes a power to me.

Romans 8:11 says, "If the Spirit of him that raised up Jesus from the dead dwell in you, he that raised up Christ from the dead shall also quicken your mortal bodies by his Spirit that dwelleth in you."

There is something in the Spirit of God that can make us immortal, and when it is taken into the heart by faith, it is the pledge of immortality.

First Corinthians 15:36 says, "That which thou sowest is not quickened, except it die."

Two years ago Dr. Waggoner stated that there was no good in any man. I remember some were talking about that statement. They brought up the case of an infidel who was kind and benevolent and wanted to know if there was not some good there. Who gave it to him? Jesus Christ. No man has anything that is good in himself.

Then what is the first step? It is to die. It is when we let our own ideas die, our own ways die, that He makes us live, that we will have a resurrection. The trouble is that we don't die; we have some of our own life to live, some of our own righteousness to patch up. In the name of the Lord, let us die! When reproof comes, let us take the reproof and die. Then we will live.

First Corinthians 15:45 says, "It is written, The first man Adam was made a living soul; the last Adam was made a quickening spirit."

Christ was made a quickening spirit. I would like to know if there is anything in this world that could ever make Christ come from the grave: it was Christ's connection with the Father. He had said, "I lay down my life, and I take it up again." In His own words, there was power to bring Him up again the third day.

Did He come up?

Yes.

Could He have lain there another day?

No, because His word had limited the time.

I am glad we have an Almighty God to trust in. I am so glad that He wants to save me and has given me this Bible and I can take it as mine, and if I do take it as mine, He will give me salvation. It is true that the Bible is good.

Another text, 1 Peter 3:18, says, "Christ also hath once suffered for sins, the just for the unjust, that he might bring us to God, being put to death in the flesh, but quickened by the Spirit."

It is an easy matter for God to do as He pleases. When we throw ourselves right in the channel of the Lord, then we have precisely what God has said. These texts are extreme texts because they tell about dead men. I tell you, when a man dies, he is dead. Seventh-day Adventists happen to believe that. But when God says, "Live," we will live because God said so.

Ephesians 2:1 says, "You hath he quickened, who were dead in trespasses and sins." It is the same power that raised Christ from the dead that quickens us and forgives our sins.

Ephesians 1:17 says, "The God of our Lord Jesus Christ, the Father of glory, may give unto you the spirit of wisdom and revelation in the knowledge of him."

I want to say right here that every person who comes to God in the way marked out in His Word will have the spirit of revelation. Do you have it? God wants you and me to have it. He wants us to have it individually, and if we do not have it, we cannot be saved. We must have the spirit of revelation.

What will this spirit do? Verses 18 through 20 say, "The eyes of your understanding being enlightened; that ye may know what is the hope of his calling, and what the riches of the glory of his inheritance in the saints, And what is the exceeding greatness of his power to us-ward who believe, according to the working of his mighty power. Which he wrought in Christ, when he raised him from the dead, and set him at his own right hand in the heavenly places."

Then what is the power that forgives our sins and enlightens our minds and sustains us?

The same power that raised Christ from the dead.

In Ezekiel 16 the Lord describes Israel's condition when they were in sin and helpless. Verses 5 and 6 say, "None eye pitied thee, to do any of these unto thee, to have compassion upon thee; but thou wast cast out in the open field, to the loathing of thy person, in the day that thou wast born. And when I passed by thee, and saw thee polluted in thine own blood, I said unto thee, . . . Live; yea, I said unto thee when thou wast in thy blood, Live."

This is the way the Lord comes to us when we are cast out to perish and there is no human help. It is then that He says to me, "Live." Then if I appropriate His Word to my heart and believe it, I will live. God says that when He comes by and sees us with no arm to save, no one to render assistance—"I said, . . . Live; yea, I said unto thee, . . . Live."

I praise God that we can live.

CHAPTER 4

The Return of Our Lord

Carlyle B. Haynes

———◆◆◆———

Carlyle Boynton Haynes (1882–1958) served the Seventh-day Adventist Church as an evangelist, administrator, and author. He worked fifteen years as an evangelist; served as president of the Greater New York Conference, the South American Division, and the Michigan Conference; directed the denomination's War Service Commission from 1940 till his death; and wrote some forty-five religious books. Haynes preached this sermon on June 14, 1946, the second Friday night of the General Conference Session held that year in Takoma Park, Maryland.

As a basis for my sermon tonight, I invite your attention to the words of our Lord regarding His second coming as they are recorded in Luke 21:25–28 from the Berkeley Version of the New Testament: "There shall also be signs in sun, moon and stars, with distress on earth among the nations, bewilderment at the roaring of sea and waves; men swooning from dread and apprehension about events that are taking place in the world; for the powers of the heavens shall be shaken. Then shall they see the Son of Man coming in a cloud with great power and glory. But when these things occur, straighten up and lift your heads because your deliverance is near."

This is counsel from the divine Head of the church. It is addressed to the servants of God in these days. It has reference to the attitude they are to take when signs heralding the Lord's return bewilder and distress those who know not God and cause them to swoon "from dread and apprehension about" the shaking of "the powers of the heavens." Instead of the people of God "swooning from dread and apprehension," they are to "straighten up and lift your heads." To the world these conditions portend the breakup of civilization and the possible suicide of the human race. To God's people they mean something quite different—"your deliverance is near."

As this General Conference draws to a close, it is fitting that we should look at the evidences that our Lord has spread before us of the certainty of one of the great articles of our faith—the nearness of our Lord's return.

The time in which we live is no ordinary time. The destiny of mankind has come to the turning point of the centuries. Universal danger is obvious to men everywhere. The world has been shocked out of its course and is in a state of convulsion. Great national and international changes have taken place. Others are in process. Still others are portending. Significant social, political, and economic developments are altering the whole appearance of human society. There have been unprecedented tempests, floods, earthquakes, famines, wars, and violence. There is unparalleled perplexity, confusion, and commotion among the nations.

The people of God, however, face the future with confidence. These developments that disturb and distress the world have not come to them unexpectedly. They have all been foretold, and their occurrence becomes a pronounced and comforting confirmation of the believers' faith and their confidence in the Word of God.

That Word explicitly foretold that the "time of the end"—the period when the Savior is to return—would be a time of abounding apostasy, skepticism, corruption, and peril. "As it was in the days of Noah, so shall it be also in the days of the Son of man." The Word also declares "the last days" would be known by great revolutionary upheavals, political and economic perplexities, and vast national and international agitations and tumults.

The Word makes plain that the last times are to be characterized by a general shaking and crumbling of the social order. "In the last days perilous times shall come." "Dreamers" were to appear who would "despise dominion, and speak evil of dignities" and "of those things which they know not" (Jude 8, 10). How true this is of our time! This is a day of great changes. Nothing must remain the same. Everything—church, religion, state, and government must be changed.

The Book of God that we have taken as our guide instructs us that when these things begin to come to pass and this time arrives, our Savior and His kingdom are at hand. Will we not, therefore, be recreant to our trust, traitors to our Lord, and merit the condemnation of being faithless watchmen if we do not go to the field—our field, the whole world—and proclaim with such power, earnestness, and conviction as we never manifested before that *the end of all things is at hand*?

All things about us today support us in such an announcement. The things our predecessors foretold on the basis of Bible prophecy and were compelled to preach by faith we can actually point to. The daily papers every morning spread before the world the certainties of our Lord's return. The radio broadcasts bring them to the attention of every home. Such terms as "the end of civilization," "the twilight of the world," "the breakup of human society," "the suicide of the human race," and "the death of the world" are today on the lips of the world's greatest scientists, thinkers, and statesmen.

Two mighty impulses

Two mighty impulses influence the minds of men around all the circle of the globe these momentous days. One is a great hope. The other is a great fear. The hope is that of a warless world, a united world, a world of human brotherhood and peace. The fear is that of world suicide and the annihilation of mankind by atomic warfare. Men have discovered how to blow the globe to pieces at the very time when they need most to learn how to hold it together.

Both the hope and the fear are set forth in Scripture as certain evidences of the end of human history. Note how the Berkeley Version of the New Testament translates 1 Thessalonians 5:1–3, "Relative to periods and dates, brothers, you need no correspondence, for you are yourselves keenly aware how the day of the Lord shall come as a thief in the night. When they shall say, 'Peace and safety,' then destruction unforeseen is on them like the birthpangs of a pregnant woman, and there will be no escape."

This means that the great hope of humanity, the United Nations, is bound to fail of its great and noble objectives. The wisdom of the world's ablest statesmen, the combined forces of religion, and the armed might of the nations are not destined to succeed. The long-desired federation of the world and parliament of man will not bring about and maintain global peace and security. This we can say by the Word of the Lord. Their aim is a lofty one, but it is not God's aim. The conception of one world is an exalted one and proceeds from the noblest of motives. It is not, however, in harmony with the purpose of God for this world in its fallen state.

The Scriptures explain the origin of nations and make plain their destiny. They make plain that the apportioning of their territories, the hidden causes of the rise and fall of kingdoms and empires, the duration of dynasties and administrations, together with the devastation of war and the deep mystery of the morale of peoples are all under the jurisdiction of the omniscient God who created, redeemed, and providentially maintains the world and the race of men upon it. Kings and emperors, dictators and tyrants, nobles and society, races and nations—the men, women, and children of the world—are all under the supervision of God and are spoken of in His inspired oracles.

In this time when the great appeal is that the peoples of the world should be *united*, it is well to keep in our thinking that it was God who "*separated* the children of men." A great cry is going up today for a *united* world. We should keep in mind that it was God who originated a *separated* world. He did not communize it. He did not bring it together. He drove it apart. He evidently perceived that it was for its own best interests that it remains apart while it continues in a state of sin.

Men have tried to unite the world before. We do well to keep in mind that it was God who brought failure, confusion, and separation to the first effort of men to build a "united nations" organization and erect a structure that would bind them together. This was at the Tower of Babel. God came down and confounded their language and separated them into all parts of the globe. He plainly meant mankind to learn by this that it was His will for them to dwell separately while sin reigns in the earth. The idea of one community of men, one family of human beings, one world is foreign to the Bible and contrary to the purpose of God for mankind while sin remains.

Human efforts to unite the nations of the world have been failures. They are bound always to be failures. It is not in God's purpose that another Tower of Babel should be erected, or, if erected, should succeed.

A perfect and permanent kingdom

Notwithstanding this inevitable failure of men, God has a plan for a perfect and permanent kingdom to take in all the earth. What man cannot do, God can and will do. His purpose is already formed. His arrangements are already perfected. The proclamation of His unchangeable purpose is being published throughout all the earth. He has His own plans. He has His own methods. He has His own time. That time is nearly here. The kingdoms of this world are soon to become the kingdom of our Lord and of His Christ, and He shall reign forever and ever.

The time is nearly here when sin is to be finally disposed of and the world freed of its curse. The time is soon to come when God's new social order will displace the wreckage of the world. The good is about to displace the evil. The blessing is about to take the place of the curse. The

Second Adam is at hand. A clean, new world is in the making. Even now all heaven may well be astir with magnificent preparation.

With Christ will come the kingdom and the glory. He will bring the cure. He will knit the broken world. He will rebuke sin and sorrow. He will banish disease and death. He will rifle the grave. He will deliver creation. He will bring permanent and worldwide recovery. He will establish eternal codes of righteousness. He will provide a just and durable peace. And on His righteous, peaceful throne He will reign forever and ever.

There is no other remedy for a ruined world than this. There is no other prospect of genuine recovery. This is the sole hope of lasting peace. It is the only hope of a sorely burdened world that under His reign will at last know the blessedness of righteous rule.

As we separate from this inspiring conference—aware that it may well be the last such conference this side of glory—and scatter to our posts of duty in all the world to resume our heralding of the Lord's return, let us realize that the swaying rush of human events and the rapidly fulfilling prophecies of God's Word make certain that we stand upon the verge of awful scenes. Stern, grim, terrible realities of blood await the world. The darker passions of mankind are awakened. There are dread possibilities in each new day. Men's hearts fail for fear of coming woes. The nations shudder with deep, convulsive dread. A sea of blood is pressing against the yielding barriers that God's mercy interposes. A rushing avalanche of wrath is impending upon the world.

While we struggle, wearied and panting amid the perils of these latter days, let us heed the words of the Captain of our salvation and be found watching. Earth's long week of toil is nearly ended. The burden is heavy, the toil intense, the struggle fierce, our duties exhausting—but the time is short.

Behind us all is dark. Around us all is gloomy. But before us, beyond the storms and tempests of divine indignation, there lies, in sunny peacefulness and rest, the glory that is to be revealed, the kingdom of the Most High, the joy unspeakable, the life eternal, the grace unsearchable—the rest that remains for the people of God.

These are the objects of our hopes, bright, glad, glowing. These are our expectations, excellent beyond any prospect earth affords. And our heart's continual longing is that the time of their coming may be hastened and that our promised inheritance may be not only certainly and surely but also speedily bestowed upon us.

Like Isaiah we cry, "Oh that thou wouldst rend the heavens, that thou wouldst come down" (Isaiah 64:1). Like Paul and his brethren, we love Christ's appearing (2 Timothy 4:8). Like the Thessalonians, we wait for the Son of God from heaven (1 Thessalonians 1:10). Like John on Patmos, we cry, "Come, Lord Jesus" (Revelation 22:20). And like the universal church, we pray, "Thy kingdom come, Thy will be done in earth, as it is in heaven" (Matthew 6:10).

Such a condition of waiting, looking, watching, expecting, hoping, anticipating, desiring, and hastening to be united with the Savior at His coming is everywhere in Scripture declared to be a characteristic of the true people of God. Therefore, the great truth we profess and carry to men everywhere demands of us a far deeper and higher consecration and devotion than that displayed by the ordinary Christian profession. It is the distinguishing mark of His true people—united with Him, eagerly awaiting His return, concerned every day to be ready to meet Him—that they become no more of this world but look out of it and away from it and truly prepare to be conveyed into another world, even that which has been promised from the beginning—Paradise restored. Nothing then satisfies them short of becoming lampbearers, instantly alert for their Lord's return. The lamp they bear is the lamp of truth, the Word of God, professed with the lips, living in the heart, manifested in all the life.

He is coming soon

The Book we love and believe tells us that Jesus will come suddenly and unexpectedly. "In such an hour as ye think not the Son of man cometh" (Matthew 24:44). When the wicked world is dreaming of pleasure, when the people are all unready, when the false cry of "peace and safety" is sounding over the earth, He will come. As the blinding glare of lightning suddenly stabs across the heavens, so Jesus will come (Matthew 24:27).

"Behold," said our Lord, "I come quickly." Christ is not only coming *sometime*. That is true, but that is not all the truth. He is coming *soon*. He is coming *quickly*. He is *at the door*. His feet are on the threshold. His hand is on the latch. Decades will not pass into centuries and centuries run on into millenniums before we witness the solemn scenes of the end.

A day will come—and soon—when the skies will disclose their glorious Maker. A day will come—and soon—when we who often watch the sky will see a cloud such as we have never seen before, a cloud made brilliantly glorious by the blazing splendor of the Son of God.

What a sight it will be! How it will thrill and enrapture the faithful ones who "love His appearing." Of a sudden the somber darkness of midnight will take on the blazing light of day, and this, in turn, will gather new brightness above all the glory of the sun and grow still more light, more bright, and more dazzling until there is revealed to us the advancing glory of the King of kings, the thrilling pageantry of the Desire of all nations. And on a glory cloud of myriads of angels, the all-conquering Christ will come again to earth.

And so we look forward to that morn of morns when once again the Lord Jesus will visit this earth. We strain to catch the first sound of His voice, that voice which will reverberate from hillside and mountaintop, echo through the silent valley, sweep across the wide and treeless plain, and pierce even to the remotest cave of the old ocean. We wait to witness the effect of that voice as it rolls through the earth, striking the shackles from grim death, breaking open the tombs of the saints, and piercing even to their dead ears. We yearn to behold the sleeping ones—awakened by that commanding Voice, feeling the thrill of life once more—raise their heads from their moldy pillows, toss aside the coverlid of dust, and spring joyfully into glorious life again.

What a vast congregation they will make as—coming from east and west, north and south, from height and depth, from land and sea, from torrid and frigid zones—they gather to greet their Redeemer, to answer the call of their Master. They will come in tremendous troops guided by angels, and sweeping upward together will take their stand on the glorious sea of glass before the throne of God.

Then, after a time, they come back to this earth made new and clean and sweet. And on this regenerated earth with the curse removed, and under new heavens clear and bright, all the righteous, with Jesus—the Son of God and the Son of man, their blessed King and Redeemer—they shall hold such a General Conference as has not entered into the thinking of men. And here on this earth we will make our eternal home.

CHAPTER 5

Woman's Work

Mrs. S. M. I. Henry

———◆◆◆———

Sarepta Myrenda (Irish) Henry (1839–1900) came to serve as a national evangelist for the Woman's Christian Temperance Union. Converted to Adventism at the Battle Creek Sanitarium, she developed the idea of a "woman ministry," which eventually resulted in the church's first organized efforts to train and support members in their parenting responsibilities. She wrote numerous articles for the Review and Herald *and published many books. Mrs. Henry preached this sermon on Sabbath, March 4, 1899, at the General Conference Session held in South Lancaster, Massachusetts.*

The greatness of my theme and of the work that God has given me would cause me to remain silent but for the fact that He is in it all. I have before me a task that would be impossible if God should not so translate to you whatever He has to say through me that we shall understand each other. But it is very necessary that we should understand each other because of the interests that are at stake.

This morning I feel led to speak concerning the necessity that is upon us as a people—the necessity that has been upon the church in every age and that God laid upon me more than twenty-five years ago but that I have never yet been able to do as I felt it should be done. I believe that I have been led toward this morning's opportunity all these years. God has at last given me an opportunity—and O how I praise Him for it! He has given me an opportunity among a people who can understand the work that came upon me as an intolerable burden more than twenty-five years ago and under which I struggled and wept and consecrated myself, starting out to do things that were impossible but that must be made possible, that must be made practical.

God has given an imperative command to the church. And what is the church? A body composed of individuals. Therefore He has spoken this command to every individual: "Go ye into all the world, and preach the gospel to every creature." And where is "every creature"? Where is that "every creature" to be found? [Voices from the congregation: In all the world.] Yes, in all the world, but somewhere else. All the world is a very big place. [Voice: Right near us.] How near? Right in your home. Everything that concerns human life anywhere must come into the world through the home. To this there is no exception. Everything good or bad that helps or hinders originates in the home. Every need of every human soul originates in the home. The salvation of the

Lord Jesus Christ as it was manifested in the earth originated in that humble home in Nazareth.

In the progress of the work of the gospel, it long ago became manifest that this "every creature" was not being reached. Something was wrong somewhere. A world was perishing in ignorance under the dispensation of a perfect gospel, and no one could discover where the lack was. About thirty years ago the burden first became so intolerable in mission fields that it could not be endured. There was a power somewhere in every heathen land that prevented the progress of the gospel. A man might acknowledge the truth of the new religion, but he was strangely hindered in living it, and it was discovered that this hindrance was to be found in the harem and zenana.* The wife and mother might be a slave, but she had the power to make it very hard for the men in her family to be Christians. She had a power that could prevent the progress of the gospel and make the work of the missionary very discouraging indeed.

I do not need to go into the story of the efforts and plans that finally resulted in the organization of work for women by women. It was recognized that the gospel could not be carried to every creature without a woman ministry—it was impossible for men to reach the women in the zenana or harem. There was a sharp and very bitter conflict in the churches over the movement to organize women's missionary societies. It was feared that these societies would draw funds and interest from the parent board. But the need was so imperative that the conflict, although sharp, was resolved decisively in favor of woman's work, and today there is no denomination other than ours that would think of doing without its organized woman's missionary work.

Twenty-five years ago we discovered that there were people in our own land who could not be reached without a woman ministry—men who were in the saloons and women known as profligates. It was the effort to reach those people who could not be reached by any other lines of effort that produced the Woman's Christian Temperance Union. The Spirit of God called that organization into existence to do a certain, specific work that, if the organization had done it, would have carried the gospel to the ends of the earth.

Psalm 68:11 contains a prophecy. It reads, "The Lord gave the word: great was the company of those that published it." In the Revised Version

---

* In India and Persia (Iran), the women's quarters in a house.

it reads, "The Lord gave the word, and the women who published it became a host." In the Jewish Bible it reads, "The Lord gave the happy tidings; and it was published by the female messengers, a numerous company." I believe that prophecy refers especially to woman's work in the church. That work still remains to be done. It must be done by women who know the truth, who have been trained in obedience to it, who can be trusted to stand against the wiles of Satan. God has made a call for a company of women who can be trusted with the very heart of the third angel's message—a company that can be trusted to stand against the perils and the temptations of these last days and take this gospel to those who cannot be reached except by a woman ministry.

The home atmosphere

As I said in the beginning, everything that is good or bad must originate in the home. For some reason the gospel has never gone as it ought to have gone. Our ministers have made confessions of weakness. Our brethren have seemed to be crippled. There has seemed to be something not discernible upon the surface that has hindered the progress of the gospel; and no matter how much you may look abroad for these things, how much these hindrances may seem to come from the world, if everything were all right in the homes that are represented by this people, the gates of hell could not prevail against you.

The hindrances are in the home, and considering the necessities that are urging us forward, it is of the first importance that we shall put forth efforts that will be adequate to meeting this need. We must do something to remove these hindrances, these defects that are in the homes, so the ministry—our brethren who are going abroad in the work—shall go out feeling strong, courageous, and refreshed. They must be removed so that every man, as he steps over his threshold and goes out to stand before the people with the gospel message, shall know that everything is all right in the homes of his people, in his own home, among his own children, in the atmosphere that he has left behind him and that he carries with him. If something in the home is continually chafing and fretting, if the children are not growing up as they ought to, if the Spirit of God does not pervade the affairs of the home, if its atmosphere is not sweet with the fragrance of heaven, how can a man go out and be strong to proclaim the gospel of Jesus? If when he arises in the pulpit to preach to his people there is trouble in his own home that is making his heart heavy and causing his brain to work all the time, how can he take up the sacred message and make it clear to the people?

In the short time since this work began, I have had a marvelous revelation through the letters that pour in upon me. I have been enabled to see into the homes of this people. The sore places in the heart of our Zion have been opened up before me, so I have come to this conference burdened. I have sat here all through it burdened for the homes that are back of us—for the people who are not here, whom you represent, whom we all represent. I have been hoping that this gospel might in some way do its full and complete work in the very center of this church.

The home is the heart of the church, and the mother in the home is its center of life. What the mother is, so is the home; and what the home is, so is the husband and father, either in his strength or in his weakness. It cannot be otherwise. He may be a man of sincere and honest purposes and with a tender heart. He may desire to do right. But if he realizes that there is something that he cannot control or cannot understand in the home life, if it is not all going smoothly as it should go, if Jesus does not live there, represented in the life of the mother and the wife in his home, he is crippled and weak in spite of all that he can do or be. God has opened up to me the necessity that there should be a work done in the homes of this and every other people, and it should originate from the women among our people.

Our women must be able to live this message of a domestic gospel, and it must be carried from our homes into other churches and out into the homes of the world. The heart of many a businessman today who professes to be an unbeliever has been turned from every tender thing that would lead him to a confession of his need simply because he feels his situation to be hopeless. He has seen how different is the home life of the men and women who profess to be Christians from that which they live before the world, and he has lost faith in the power of Christianity. He says, "It fails in the home—the place where I would like to have Christ manifested." Failure there is failure everywhere. Many a man has said to me, "If I could only see Christianity manifested in the home life so that the home of the minister, the home of the man and woman who profess to be Christians, should be in harmony with their profession, I would be glad to seek it and to accept it." Before the gospel can be taken to every creature, those who go forth from this church must be equipped with it.

It will not be very long—the time is even now here—before such a strong light will shine upon those who represent this work before the world that their every act will tell for or against the truth. Every home must be able to stand the test when it is criticized, when the world shall turn its telescope upon it and analyze it. It must find the mother a true representative of Jesus Christ, the home atmosphere permeated with the very fragrance of heaven, and the influences scattered abroad by the children and all who pass in and out over the threshold such as shall tell for Christ.

A highly favored people

Seventh-day Adventists are a highly favored people. At first I believed them a perfect people. With longing eye I looked upon those who had been brought up in these great principles. I envied them because of the high point of privilege that they occupied. I thought every member of the church must be true because it cost so much to become a Seventh-day Adventist. It must take all of self out of any man. I could see nothing to motivate one to join this people other than an unconditional surrender to truth—a fidelity to truth that would lead to a renunciation of everything fleshly, everything not of Christ.

I believe that this view of what Seventh-day Adventists must be is just what God intends they shall be. I don't think I imputed one thing in the line of perfection to this people that God does not intend they shall reach. Since my life and my heart have been knit together with you in these bonds of Christian fellowship and labor, I have come to feel that we are all called together to those heights of attainment that mean perfectness in Christ, perfectness in everything that belongs to the outgrowth and development of character. The world has a right to call upon us for perfectness. So, in order that we may be able to meet the expectations of God and a lost world, a great work must be done in our homes.

By nothing have I been kept so busy since I came among this people as by the inquiries of fathers and mothers as to how they can correct the living of their children. "What can I do with my boy?" writes a father to me, and then he will go on to say that his boy is fifteen or sixteen years old and has already begun to slip away. He is out on the street, has begun to form associations with street boys, to smoke cigarettes, to use bad language. He has become unmanageable. What shall be done with him?

"Why won't my child obey me?" is the cry that comes continually from fathers and mothers. I cannot go into the discussion of the why of all this in detail, but I will indicate what is at the root of the whole matter. If it does not apply to you personally, it applies to somebody whom you ought to reach with the truth: the child in the home deals by his father and mother and the principles they represent precisely as you—the father and the mother—deal by your heavenly Father and the principles that He represents. There is no deviation from this rule. I know that this is a hard thing to say, but it is even harder to live with this fact.

Every child is a publisher. A family of children is a publishing association. The children publish that which is supposed to be secret in the life of the father and mother. That which has been uttered in the secret heart of the parents, that which is supposed to be hidden within the four walls of the home is taken abroad and published upon the street corners by what the children are.

A recent letter

Yesterday I opened a letter addressed to me that one sister wrote on behalf of another. A mother and father whose hearts were breaking were too heartsick and sore themselves to write to me, and so this friend wrote for them, telling me about their boy. He had been a good, kind, gentle boy in the home; but she says a change is coming over him. He says that he "has got to begin to do for himself pretty soon, and that he does not see how he can do for himself, and keep the Sabbath." Then this sister cries, "O, I am so discouraged! I am so disheartened. How can we preserve our young people against the day of our Lord's coming?"

That is the cry. The obligation is upon this people to preserve their children unto the Lord's coming. How shall we answer for our children? If the Lord comes and finds that our children are not with us, how shall we answer when our names are called in the judgment? How will our case stand if we cannot say, "Here am I, and the children whom Thou hast given me"?

I replied, "Tell those parents that their boy ought never to have been left to think for one moment of such a thing as 'striking out for himself.' " What does it mean to "strike out for himself"? It means a repudiation of the whole obligation of the individual to Christ. Every effort that is made by a Christian man to earn a living is a repudiation of Christ. Every thought of earning a living is a repudiation of Christ. And when that thought is in the heart of the father and the mother, it is a thistle seed out of which will grow a whole harvest of thistles.

"To earn a living"! I presume if I should go out among the people in this congregation, I would find scores who are burdened this Sabbath morning as to just how they are going to get along next week in the effort to earn a living. I want to tell you that there is nothing in the world so hard for a Christian man as to earn a living, because God is not in it. He will not help him at all. He must fight God every step of the way if he undertakes to earn a living. He is here in this world for another purpose, and that purpose was indicated in the purpose for which Christ came into the world.

What did Christ come for? To seek and to save that which was lost. If you read in the First Epistle of John, fourth chapter, seventeenth verse, you will find this: "as he is, so are we in this world." So we are here for no other purpose than to try to bring back to God that which Satan stole away from Him. Each one is to help every other to get back to God, to bring the home back to the plane upon which it was started, to bring the business of the world up to the level of the gospel, to be true representatives of Jesus in every walk of life. We are here for that one purpose and for no other, and God intends that we shall use everything that comes into our lives—the affairs of this world, the material things about us—simply as opportunities for manifesting Christ, for witnessing for Him by the power of the Holy Spirit.

God has set us in families for that purpose. He has placed men and women together in the relationship of husband and wife and parents and children that there might be that intimate and close relation that would make it possible for the unity of the Spirit in the bond of peace to be illustrated—to become a living reality to the glory of God. He has placed fathers, mothers, and children in that intimate and close relation that the children might be shaped, developed, educated, built up, and made able to go out into the world and take it just as Satan changed it, all its very worst; and instead of being overcome by it, to overcome it, subdue it, and bring back for the use of God at least one little section of the world redeemed from the curse.

God's object in the home

The home was God's first institution. He created it, like a machine, for a certain, specific, and definite work. He gave it its work, and for that work He set apart a certain proportion of power. Every good machinist, in making provision to apply power, will take into consideration three things: the work to be done, the amount and kind of work that the machine is to do, and the application of power according to that work. Then he takes into consideration the friction in the machine, and he makes provision for the application of power enough over and above what is required for the work to overcome the friction. He also takes into consideration what must be left in reserve to meet emergencies.

Now God is just that kind of machinist. The work to be done by the home is the production of men and women who should be able to go out into the world and take it just as they found it, and instead of being overcome by it, to subdue and overcome it. God never intended that any boy or girl should go out of a Christian home and go to ruin. Never! He made provision to apply sufficient power for the home to do its appointed work. Then He took into account the friction: He weighed an evil heredity clear back to Adam. He took it up and weighed and measured it. He knew just what part it was going to play in the life of that child. He took up the evil influences that might be in the environment. He took up the temperament of the father and the mother. And He took up the saloon down on the corner and the house of sin and all the evil things that Satan could possibly bring to bear.

I do not believe that God was ever taken by surprise by one thing that Satan did. He knew everything that the saloon meant to your boy and what all the evil influences of the world meant to every boy and girl in any Christian home. He knew all about it, and in the face of all these things He dared to say one thing to parents that is full of hope and inspiration and courage. In the second chapter of Acts we read concerning that wonderful manifestation of the Holy Spirit that is to come upon the church—the outpouring of the fullness of the Holy Spirit: "Repent, and be baptized every one of you in the name of Jesus Christ for the remission of sins, and ye shall receive the gift of the Holy Ghost. For the promise is unto you, and to your children, and to all that are afar off, even as many as the LORD our God shall call" (verses 38, 39).

The promise of the Holy Ghost is to you and to your children. This states plainly that there shall be sufficient power to run this machinery of the home so that the children who go out of it shall be able to act like true and reliable men and women; they shall be able to go into the world and stand for the truth.

Just think what it would be to this message if our children, as they go among their young companions in school and in the work of life, should second the message that the father preaches on the Sabbath day from the pulpit, so that people might say, "I believe in that man's preaching because I know his children." "I believe in that woman's testimony because I know her home, because I know her children." Do you not think this would help in the work of spreading the message?

I want to tell you that it is possible even now to do a work that will bring back the children who have gone astray. That is the thing, my brethren and sisters, upon which I have set my heart. The burden that is upon my soul in this day is that there shall be revived in the homes of this people a power that shall bring the children back by the force of the love of the truth—the force of God that is in it. But before that can be done, a work must be done for and by the mother.

I have had letters from mothers who were upon the verge of suicide. More than one mother has written to me, "Your letter came just in time. I was so discouraged." I have had letters from women who had already, in their discouragement, begun to slip down that incline that leads to unbelief and infamy. You and I may not know just what it means to be caught in such a fog, but the very fact that any poor soul could be so caught has aroused all the sympathies of my heart. I said years ago that I will by the grace of God keep my heart alive and quick to any such need as that and that I will answer that need to every extent of my ability. That is why I am here, and that is why God gave me this work—because He knew that my heart is alive to these things.

One thing is apparent to me. I have been seeking for a solution to the problem of these conditions. The question is, How can such things be among a people with such principles? This is the answer that has come to me: as the sweetest things, when they turn sour, become the most offensive, so to turn against the greatest light and truth is to fall into the greatest darkness and evil. This people has had wonderful light. All through the years the light has been pouring in upon this people. Yet there are invalids, physical and moral, among us. This is to be accounted for by the fact that we have not walked in the light that God has given us. The truth has been held in unrighteousness, and to hold any truth in unrighteousness is to make poison of it. The one thing that is before us as a people is to look everything squarely in the face in the clear light that God has given us and try to get ourselves ready to meet every emergency and every need so that we may be ready to go out into the field and do the work that belongs to us to do.

CHAPTER 6

The Third Angel's Message

A. T. Jones

———◆◆◆———

Alonzo T. Jones (1850–1923) began preaching for the Seventh-day Adventist Church in 1873. Twelve years later, he and Ellet J. Waggoner became coeditors of Signs of the Times. *These two men stirred the Adventist Church with the message of righteousness by faith that they brought to the 1888 General Conference Session in Minneapolis. Jones served as editor of the* Review and Herald *from 1897 to 1901 and wrote voluminously. Eventually, however, his involvement with Dr. J. H. Kellogg led him to cut his ties with the church. Jones preached this sermon on Sunday, February 26, 1893, at the General Conference Session held that year in Battle Creek, Michigan. The sermon was the eighteenth in a series titled "The Third Angel's Message."*

One of the main points of the study tonight is to see what place the law of God occupies in the subject of righteousness by faith; what place the law of God occupies in our obtaining righteousness by Jesus Christ alone; what proof the Lord has given us so that we can have the confidence to claim by faith the promise of the Holy Spirit.

Romans chapter five, verse twenty: "Moreover the law entered, that the offence might abound." In other words—words with which you are all familiar—"by the law is the knowledge of sin" (Romans 3:20). Why was the law given? What was the first purpose of its giving? [Congregation: "To show us what sin is."] To make sin abound; to give the knowledge of sin. So, "the law entered, that the offence might abound"; that sin might appear as it is.

In the seventh chapter of Romans, verses twelve and thirteen, Paul tells us how it appeared to him: "Wherefore the law is holy, and the commandment holy, and just, and good. Was then that which is good made death unto me? God forbid. But sin, that it might appear sin, working death in me by that which is good; that sin *by the commandment* might become *exceeding sinful*" (emphasis added). Then, to make sin abound and make it appear as it is, exceeding sinful—that is the first object of the giving of the law, isn't it?

Now let us read right on in Romans chapter five: "Moreover the law entered, that the offence might abound. But where sin abounded, grace did much more abound" (verse 20). Then did the law come alone, making sin to appear alone? [Congregation: "No."] It is simply the means to another end—the means to an end by which to attain another object beyond the knowledge of sin. Is that so? [Congregation: "Yes."] So then, where sin abounds, where is it that grace

68

abounds? [Congregation: "In the same place."] Right there? [Congregation: "Yes."]

But does it read that way: "Where sin abounded, grace abounded"? [Congregation: "No; 'much more.' "] That would be pretty good wouldn't it, if it was only where sin abounds there grace abounds? That would be pretty good. But that is not the way the Lord does things, you know. He does things absolutely well. "Where sin abounded, grace did much *more* abound." [Congregation: "Amen."] Then, brethren, when the Lord, by His law, has given us the knowledge of sin, just at that very moment, at that very point, *grace* is *much more abundant* than the knowledge of sin. Is that so? [Congregation: "Yes."]

So, we have found this much: that when the law gives the knowledge of sin, at that particular moment and in that very place, the grace of God is much more abundant than the knowledge of sin. But when the law gives the knowledge of sin, what puts the *conviction* there? [Congregation: "The Spirit of God."]

Before we read the passage that tells us about the Spirit, however, let us see what we are to get from what we have read so far. What are you and I henceforth to get from the knowledge of sin? [Congregation: "Abundance of grace."] Then there is no place for discouragement at the sight of sins anymore, is there? [Congregation: "No."] No possibility of that. It is impossible, you see, for you or me to get discouraged or under a cloud anymore at the knowledge of sin because no matter how many sins are brought to our knowledge, why, right there, in those very things and at that very time in our experience, the grace of God abounds much more than all the knowledge of sins.

I say again, how is it possible for us ever to be discouraged? Brethren, isn't it so that the Lord wants us to be of good cheer? [Congregation: "Amen!"]

The Comforter

Well now, this passage that we have before us brings the same thing to view. John 16:7 says, "Nevertheless I tell you the truth . . ." What is He telling us? [Congregation: "Truth."] Good! And He told us also that "ye shall know the truth, and the truth shall make you free" (John 8:32). That is it then, isn't it? "Nevertheless I tell you the truth; It is expedient for you that I go away: for if I go not away, the Comforter will not come unto you" (John 16:7).

Who will not come? [Congregation: "The Comforter."] Who? [Congregation: "The Comforter."] The Comforter? Is that His name? Is that what He is—the Comforter? [Congregation: "Yes."]

"But if I depart, I will send him unto you. And when *he* is come . . ." (verses 7, 8, emphasis added). Who has come? [Congregation: "The Comforter."] "And when he is come, he will reprove [or convince] the world of sin" (verse 8). Who does it? [Congregation: "The Comforter."] Is it the Comforter who convinces of sin? [Congregation: "Yes."] Is He the Comforter *when He does it?* [Congregation: "Yes."]

Now, each one wants to get hold of that. Is not He the Reprover when He convinces us of sin and the Comforter some other time? [Congregation: "No."] It is the *Comforter* who *reproves,* thank the Lord! Then what are we to get out of the reproof of sin? [Congregation: "Comfort."] Whose comfort? [Congregation: "The Lord's comfort."] The comfort we get comforts us just at the time when it is needed. Then where is the room for our getting discouraged any more at the knowledge of sin? Isn't that the very thought we have read in the fifth chapter of Romans?

So, just at the moment and at that time and at the place where sin abounds, there grace much more abounds. And just at the time when the Holy Spirit is giving conviction of sin, He is the Comforter. Don't you see then that in all that we have an everlasting victory over Satan?

Does Satan get the advantage of that man who believes God right then? No. Satan comes and says, "See what a sinner you are." But, thank the Lord, "where sin [abounds], grace [does] much more abound." [Congregation: "Amen!"]

"Well," says another, "I have such a deep conviction of sin. It seems to me I was never convicted of sin so deeply before in all my life." Thank the Lord, we have got more comfort than ever before in our lives. Don't you see, brethren, that this is so? [Congregation: "It is so."] Well then, let us thank the Lord for that. I should like to know why we should not praise the Lord right along.

We have found that the law makes sin abound in order that grace may abound so that we may be led to Christ. But there is more in Romans 5:20. Now what are the two things together for—the law making sin abound in order that more grace may abound? What are they together for? "That as sin hath reigned unto death . . ." We know that's so, don't we? Now that is so. The law makes sin abound *that* we may be led to more abundance of grace *in order* "*that* as sin hath reigned unto death, even so might grace reign."

What does "even so" mean? Just as certainly. Just so. Then, isn't it true that God will make that abundance of grace to reign in our lives just as certainly as ever sin did in the world? [Congregation: "Yes, sir."] But, mark you, when the grace much more bountifully reigns, then what is the comparison between freedom from sin now and the slavery to it before? The freedom is much more abundant even than the slavery was. "That *as sin hath reigned* unto death, *even so* might *grace reign* through *righteousness* unto *eternal life* by *Jesus Christ* our Lord" (verse 21, emphasis added).

Now let us see the whole story. "The law entered, that the offence might abound" in order that we might find the more abundant grace abounding right there in all those places. And the grace abounds "through righteousness unto eternal life by Jesus Christ our Lord." Then what did the law enter for? [Voice: "To bring us to Christ."] Yes. Don't you see? Then whenever anybody in this world uses the Ten Commandments for any purpose other than to reach Jesus Christ, what kind of a purpose is he putting them to? [Congregation: "A wrong purpose."] He is perverting the intent of God in giving the law, isn't he? [Congregation: "Yes, sir."] To use the law of God for any other purpose than that men may reach Christ Jesus is to use the law in a way that God never intended it to be used.

So, the law brings us to Christ. That's certain. What for? [Congregation: "That we may be justified."] What does the law want of you and me before we reach Jesus Christ? When the law finds us, does it want anything from us? [Congregation: "It wants righteousness."] What kind? [Congregation: "Perfect righteousness."] Whose? [Congregation: "God's."] God's righteousness? [Congregation: "Yes."] Just such righteousness as God alone manifests in His own life, in His own way of doing things? [Congregation: "Yes."] Will the law be content with anything less than that from you and me? Will it accept anything a hair's breadth less than that? [Congregation: "No."] If we could come within a hair's breadth of it, that's too far short. We miss it.

What the law wants

Turn to First Timothy, chapter one, verse five. There, Paul tells us what the law wants *out* of you and me, and what it wants *in* us, too. "Now the end [the object, the aim, the intent, the purpose] of the commandment is charity." What is charity? [Congregation: "Love."] What kind of love? [Congregation: "The love of God."] "Out of a pure heart." Out of what kind of a heart? [Congregation: "A pure heart."] "And of a good conscience." What kind of a conscience? [Congregation: "Good."] "And of faith unfeigned." That is what the law wants to find in you and me, isn't it? Will it accept you and me with anything less than that which it demands—perfect love, manifested "out of a pure heart, and of a good conscience, and of faith unfeigned"? No, never. Well, it is simply demanding *perfection.*

Have we—has any man in the world—any of that kind of love to offer to the law of God? [Congregation: "No."] Has any man naturally that kind of a conscience? [Congregation: "No."] Has he that kind of faith? [Congregation: "No."] No, sir. So, the law makes that demand of every man on the earth tonight no matter who he is. It makes it of you and me. It makes that demand of people in Africa and of all the people on the earth. And it will not accept anything less than that from any of them.

But we are talking about ourselves tonight. So, the law comes to you and me and says, "I want charity; I want perfect love—the love of God. I want to see it in your life all the time. And I want to see it manifested out of a pure heart and through a good conscience and unfeigned faith." That is where we are.

"Well," says one, "I've done my best, but I don't have it." But the law will say, "That isn't what I want. I don't want your best; I want perfection. It isn't your righteousness that I am after; I want God's righteousness from you. It isn't your doing that I want; it is God's doing in your life." That is what the law says to every man.

When I am shut off thus at the very first question even when I said I did my best, then I have nothing more to say. Is that not what Scripture says, "That every mouth may be stopped"? (Romans 3:19). It does just that, does it not? But there comes a still, small Voice saying, "Here is perfect life. Here is the life of God. Here is a pure heart. Here is a good conscience. Here is unfeigned faith." Where does that Voice come from? [Congregation: "Christ."] Ah, the Lord Jesus Christ, who in the flesh in which I live came and stood where I stand. He lived there. The perfect love of God was manifested there. Perfect purity of heart was manifested there. A good conscience was manifested there. And the unfeigned faith of the mind that was in Jesus Christ is there.

Well then, Christ simply comes and tells me, "Here, take this." That will satisfy, then, will it? [Congregation: "Yes."] The life manifested in Jesus Christ, that will satisfy the law. The purity of heart that Jesus Christ gives, that will satisfy the law. The good conscience that He can create, that will satisfy. The unfeigned faith that He gives, that will satisfy. Will it? [Congregation: "Yes."]

Is that not what the law wants all the time? It is Jesus Christ that the law wants, is it not? [Congregation: "Yes."] That is what the law wants. That is the same thing called for in the fifth chapter of Romans, is it not? But why does it call for it in connection with me? It calls for Christ in me because the law wants to see that thing *in me*. Then is not the object of the law of God the gospel of Christ alone? "Christ in you the hope of glory"? (Colossians 1:27). Ah, that is so.

Romans 5:1, 5 says that when we are justified by faith, we have peace with God through our Lord Jesus Christ, and the love of God is shed abroad in our hearts by the Holy Ghost which is given unto us. And that is charity—supreme love. Acts 15:8, 9 says, "And God, which knoweth the hearts, bare them witness, giving them the Holy Ghost, even as he did unto us; and put no difference between us and them, *purifying their hearts by faith*" (emphasis added). There is the love of God out of a pure heart. Hebrews 9:14 says, "How much more shall the blood of Christ, who through the eternal Spirit offered himself without spot to God, purge your conscience from dead works to serve the living God?" There is a clean conscience, brethren; there is the love of God out of a good conscience.

Then that faith that He gives—the faith of Jesus that enables us to keep the commandments of God—there is the love of God by a faith unfeigned. Oh, then the message of the righteousness of God that is by faith in Jesus Christ brings us to and brings to us the perfect fulfillment of the law of God, does it not? [Congregation: "Yes."] Then that is the object and the aim and the one single point of the third angel's message, is it not? [Congregation: "Yes."] That is Christ—Christ in His righteousness, Christ in His purity, Christ in His love, Christ in His gentleness, Christ in His entire being, Christ and Him crucified. That is the

Word, brethren; let us be glad of it. Let us be glad of it. [Congregation: "Amen."]

So, when we have Jesus, when we have received Him by faith and the law stands before us or we stand before it and it makes its wondrous demand of charity, we can say, "Here it is; it is in Christ, and He is mine! 'A good conscience'—the blood of Christ has created it in me; here it is. 'Faith unfeigned'—He has given it to me; here it is." Then, just as *Steps to Christ* tells us, we can come to Jesus now and be cleansed and stand before the law without one touch of shame or remorse. Brethren, when I have that which makes me at perfect agreement with the law of God, then I am satisfied and cannot help but be glad that I am satisfied.

Righteousness without the law

Now let us turn and read the third chapter of Romans. Simply reading Romans 3:19–22 tells the whole story: "Now we know that what things soever the law saith, it saith to them who are under the law: that every mouth may be stopped, and all the world may become guilty before God." Is that not so? That which tells me that I am a sinner cannot tell me that I am righteous. "But now . . ." When? [Congregation: "Now."] "But now the righteousness of God without the law is manifested." That is so, is it not? [Congregation: "Yes."] The law cannot manifest it in us because we cannot see it there. Sin has so blinded and corrupted us that we cannot see it in the law, and if we could see it there, we could not get it there because there is nothing in us to start with that is fit for it. We are utterly helpless.

So now, "the righteousness of God without the law is manifested. . . . Even the righteousness of God which is by faith of Jesus Christ unto all and upon all them that believe." What does that word *believe* mean when God speaks it? [Congregation: "Faith."] And what is genuine faith? Submission of the will to Him. A yielding of the heart to Him. A fixing of the affections upon Him. That is what He means here to those who will receive Him, because *believing* is receiving when God speaks. He says so in the first chapter of John, verse twelve: "But as many as *received* him, to them gave he power to become the sons of God, even to them that *believe* on his name" (emphasis added). "Even the righteousness of God which is by faith of Jesus Christ unto all and upon all them that believe: for there is no difference" (Romans 3:22). Then everyone here can have it tonight? *Can* have it? *Do* have it, because we believe it.

Well now, that is the object of the law, is it not—to bring us to Jesus Christ that we may be justified by faith, made righteous by faith, that His righteousness—the righteousness of God in Christ—may be ours? That is it. Well, when that is true, when we have got there, *then* what is the use of the law? Then what is the law for? [Congregation: "It witnesses."] Let us read now the part of the twenty-first verse that I didn't read: "But now the righteousness of God without the law is manifested, *being witnessed by the law*" (emphasis added). That is as far as we need to read just now. When the law gives a knowledge of sin in order that we may have the knowledge of the abundance of grace to take away the sin, then grace reigns through righteousness unto eternal life by Jesus Christ. And this righteousness of God by faith in Christ is our own through the working of the law. The knowledge of sin has brought us to Christ, and now we have Him, and the law is satisfied as to all the demands that it has made upon us.

When the law of God has made demands upon us that we cannot satisfy by any other possible means except by Jesus Christ being present in ourselves, then will it stand right there and say, "That is right, and I am satisfied with it"? [Congregation: "Yes."] Then, if anybody begins to question it and says, "It is not so," we have witnesses to prove it, have we?

Now you see this: that it is necessary for several reasons that we should have witnesses. One reason is this: when God speaks and we believe it, then we know, each one for himself, that the righteousness of God is our own, that we are entitled to it, that it belongs to us, and that we can rest in perfect peace upon it. But there are other people who need to know this too. Can they know it by my saying that it is so? Will that convince them? Is that proof enough to them? [Congregation: "No."] They need something better even than my word. The Lord has met that very demand and has given us witnesses to whom they can appeal. They can ask these witnesses whenever they please whether or not what we have is genuine. Is that so? [Congregation: "Yes."]

If they inquire of us, we can tell them what the Lord has told us to say. If that is not enough, they can ask those witnesses. We can say, "I have some friends who have known me from my birth. They know me all the way through. They know me better than I do myself, and if you want more than what I say, go and ask them; they'll tell you."

How many of these friends are there? [Congregation: "Ten."] Is their word worth anything? Do they tell the truth?

Ah, they are truth itself (Psalm 119:142). In bearing witness, it is impossible for them to testify other than the truth. When they say, "This life is well pleasing to me," that demand is satisfied. That is enough for anybody in the universe, is it not? [Congregation: "Yes."]

So then, the man who claims to believe in Jesus and claims the righteousness of God that comes to the believer in Jesus, is his claiming it enough for this world? [Congregation: "No."] There are lots of men who will say it, "Why yes, we believe in the Savior. I have a right to claim, too, the righteousness that He has—perfect holiness and perfect sanctification. I have not sinned for ten years and am above all temptation, and I know it."

How do you know it?

"Why, I feel it in my heart and have for several years."

That is no evidence at all, for "the heart is deceitful above all things, and desperately wicked" (Jeremiah 17:9).

Deceitful above *how* many things? [Congregation: "All things."] All things? [Congregation: "Yes."] Above Satan even? [Congregation: "Yes."] Is the heart actually deceitful above all things? [Congregation: "Yes."] It is more deceitful than Satan himself, isn't it? [Congregation: "Yes."] The heart will deceive me quicker and more often than Satan will.

When that person *feels it in his heart,* is that a good kind of evidence? When my heart says that I am good, then what is it doing? [Congregation: "It is deceiving."] Solomon said, "He that trusteth his own heart is a fool." Therefore, we cannot afford to trust such things as a man's feelings on such an important question as this. No sir, we need better evidence than a man's heart gives us that he has the righteousness of God and is fit for the judgment and that he hasn't sinned for ten years; that he is holy and sanctified and above temptation, etc., etc. We need something better than that. And if that person who claims to have the righteousness of God by faith in Jesus Christ has only that for a witness, what is his claim worth? [Congregation: "Nothing at all."] Just nothing at all. It is a deceptive claim; he never can rely upon it.

Witnessed by the law

But the Lord has not left us there. When we want to know that these things are so in our experience, we are not to look within but to look at what God says to see whether it is so. When we have found Jesus Christ, then the Lord doesn't want us to look within to see whether He is there. He has furnished us witnesses whose testimony will tell us all the time that He is there, and these witnesses will tell everybody else that He is there. The righteousness of God is now manifested, which is by faith of Jesus Christ, and when it is, it is witnessed *by the law*.

Then the law is, first, to bring us unto Christ, and after it has led us to Christ and we have found Him, then it witnesses that that is what has actually happened. So, first, it gives the knowledge of sin, and second, it witnesses to the righteousness of God that is by faith.

Well then, when any man or angel uses the law of God for anything other than these two purposes, what is he doing with the law of God? [Congregation: "Perverting it."] He is perverting the whole thing. He is using it for purposes for which God never intended it at all.

Where is our righteousness from? [Congregation: "God."] "Their righteousness is of me, saith the LORD" (Isaiah 54:17). "For God, who commanded the light to shine out of darkness, hath shined in our hearts, to give the light of the knowledge of the glory of God in the face of Jesus Christ" (2 Corinthians 4:6). Where do we find the knowledge of the glory of God? [Congregation: "In the face of Jesus Christ."]

Now let's read 2 Corinthians 3:18: "But we all, with open face beholding as in a glass the glory of the Lord, are changed into the same image from glory to glory, even as by the Spirit of the Lord." Then what is it that we see in the face of Jesus Christ? [Congregation: "The glory of the Lord."] What is the glory of the Lord? We have read here, we have been told here by the Spirit of God that the message of the righteousness of God that is by faith of Jesus Christ is the beginning of the glory that is to lighten the whole earth. Then what is the glory of God? His righteousness. His character. Where do we find it? In Jesus Christ. The glory of God is revealed in the face of Jesus Christ. He said so, you see, so that is where we look for it.

Do we look to the law for righteousness? [Congregation: "No."] Even after we have been brought to Christ, do we look there for righteousness? [Congregation: "No."] Where do we look for righteousness? In the face of Jesus Christ. There "we all, with open face beholding as in a glass the glory of the Lord, are changed into the same image from glory to glory"—from righteousness to righteousness, from character to character, from goodness to goodness, even as by the Spirit of the Lord.

Don't you see how the righteousness of God and the Holy Spirit go hand in hand? Don't you see that when we obtain the righteousness that is by faith of Jesus Christ, the blessing of Abraham indeed, that then the Holy Spirit cannot be kept away from us? You cannot separate the two; they belong together. When we have that and know we have it by faith in His word, then He says we have a right to ask for the Holy Spirit and to receive it, too.

Why, look at it—He came "to redeem them that were under the law, that we might receive the adoption of sons. And because ye are sons, *God hath sent* forth the Spirit of his Son into your hearts" (Galatians 4:5, 6, emphasis added). He *sends* it. He doesn't want to hold it back; He *sends* it into the heart. It is a free gift.

Don't you see that it is impossible to keep the righteousness of God and the Holy Spirit separate? So when we are "changed into the same image from glory to glory, even as by the Spirit of the Lord" and when the image of God in Jesus Christ is found in us, what then? There is the impress, the seal of God. When by looking into the face of Jesus Christ—and there alone—we have received the righteousness of God that is by faith in Him, we are changed into the same image. The effect is to restore the image of God in us by the working of the Spirit of God upon the soul. When that is done, then the same Spirit is there to affix the seal of the living God—the eternal impress of His own image.

After we have come to Christ, we don't look into the law for righteousness. Where do we look? [Congregation: "In the face of Jesus Christ."] Into the face of Jesus Christ. And while we look there, what does the law say? [Congregation: "That is right."] The law testifies, "That is the place to look. That is what I want you to have. That is satisfactory. We are perfectly agreed."

The tabernacle of witness

When the people of Israel sinned and did something against the commandments of the Lord, they were to bring a sacrifice, and its blood was offered, atonement was made, and they were forgiven (Leviticus 4). *Then* as *now,* the commandments witnessed to the righteousness that they obtained by faith in Jesus. Therefore, the tabernacle was called "the tabernacle of *witness*" (Acts 7:44; Numbers 17:7, 8; 18:2). The tabernacle of the testimony is the same thing because testimony is the evidence given by a witness. So the tabernacle was the tabernacle of witness or testimony, and the ark was the ark of the testimony or witness because it contained the tables of the testimony. The tables of stone, the tables of the law, were the tables of the *testimony,* because they were the evidence of the witness that God appointed to witness to His righteousness, which comes without the law, by faith in Jesus Christ alone. Then it is everlastingly true throughout the universe that "if righteousness come by the law, then Christ is dead in vain" (Galatians 2:21). Forever and everywhere it is true that "their righteousness is of me, saith the Lord." And the law witnesses to the righteousness that all obtain from God without the law but by Jesus Christ.

Then isn't it true, as I said a while ago, that whether man or angel uses the law of God for any other than these two purposes, he perverts the law of God entirely from what God intended. So, the righteousness of God that is by faith of Jesus Christ satisfies everything, does it not? Everything *now* and for how long? [Congregation: "Forever."] Now and evermore it satisfies everything. Then, by the evidences that God gave us, which are everlastingly sure, we may know for our own selves that it is ours. By the witnesses that God has given, everybody in the world may know that we are entitled to it. This is to fit us for the seal of God, the righteousness of God, in order that through this we may be changed into the same image. And when that is completed, what then? What witnesses to that? [Congregation: "The Sabbath of the Lord."] It will witness to that finished, completed work all the way through.

The presence of Christ makes holy and sanctifies the place where He is. When Christ is present somewhere in His fullness, then that place is sanctified. What is the sign of sanctification? [Congregation: "The Sabbath."] And sanctification complete is God's complete work in the soul. When the work of God is completed in the soul, the law of God will witness to it all the way. But what part of the law of God is a witness to that particular thing, the complete sanctification of His people? [Congregation: "The Sabbath of the Lord."] It stands there as the chief witness, and the seal is affixed. That work is completed.

Brethren, are we not right now in the time of the sealing? [Congregation: "Yes."] And that sealing is through the righteousness of God that is by faith of Jesus Christ, is it not? And when that seal is received, when it is affixed there, then these can stand through the time of the plagues, through all the temptations and trials of Satan when he works with all power and signs and lying wonders. For the promise is "because thou hast kept the word of my patience, I also will keep thee from the hour of temptation, which shall come upon all the world, to try them that dwell upon the earth" (Revelation 3:10).

And when that is past—then entrance into the heavenly city; entrance into the heavenly city. Thank the Lord! We are to pass through some tests. But, brethren, when we have this righteousness of Jesus Christ, we have that which will pass through every test.

In that day there will be two parties. Some will be there when the door is shut, and they will want to go in. They will say, "Lord, open to us. We want to come in." And He will ask, "What have you done that you should come in? What right have you to enter the inheritance here? What claim have you upon that?"

"Oh, we are acquainted with Thee. We have eaten and drunk in Thy presence, and Thou hast taught in our streets. And we have prophesied in Thy name, and in Thy name we have done many wonderful works. Lord, is not that evidence enough? Open the door."

What is the answer? "Depart from me, ye that work iniquity." What did they say? "We have done many wonderful works. *We* are just exactly right. *We* are righteous. Therefore *we* have a right to be there. Open the door."

But *we* doesn't count there, does it?

Another company

Another company will be there that day—a great multitude that no man can number—all nations, and kindred, and tongues, and people. And they will come up to enter in. And if anyone should ask them, "What have you done that you should enter here? What claim have you here?" the answer will be, "I haven't done anything at all to deserve it. I am a sinner dependent only on the grace of the Lord. Oh, I was so wretched and in such bondage that nobody could deliver me but the Lord Himself. I was so miserable that all I could ever do was to have the Lord constantly to comfort me. I was so poor that I had constantly to beg from the Lord. So blind that no one but the Lord could cause me to see. So naked that no one could clothe me but the Lord himself. All the claim that I have is what Jesus has done for me.

"But the Lord has loved me. When in my wretchedness I cried, He delivered me. When in my misery I wanted comfort, He comforted me all the way. When in my poverty I begged, He gave me riches. When in my blindness I asked Him to show me the way, He led me all the way and made me to see. When I was so naked that no one could clothe me, why, He gave me this garment that I have on. All that I have to present as that by which I can enter is just what He has done for me. If that will not pass me through, then I am left out. That will be just too. If I am left out, I have no complaint to make. But, oh, will not this entitle me to enter and possess the inheritance?"

But he says, "Well, there are some very particular persons here. They want to be fully satisfied with everybody who passes through this door. We have ten examiners here. When they look into a man's case and say that he is all right, why then he can pass. Are you willing that these shall be called to examine your case?" And we shall answer, "Yes, yes. I want to enter in, and I am willing to submit to any examination. Even if I am left out, I have no complaint to make. I am lost anyway when I am left to myself."

"Well," says he, "we will call them then." And so those ten are brought up, and they say, "Why yes, we are perfectly satisfied with him. Why, yes, the deliverance that he obtained from his wretchedness is that which our Lord wrought. The comfort that he had all the way and that he needed so much is that which our Lord gave. The wealth that he has, whatever he has, poor as he was, the Lord gave it. He was blind; whatever he sees, it is the Lord who gave it to him. He sees only what is the Lord's. And naked as he was, that garment that he has on, the Lord gave it to him. The Lord wove it, and it is all divine. It is only Christ. Why, *yes, he can come in!*"

[Here the congregation began singing,

Jesus paid it all,
All to Him I owe;
Sin had left a crimson stain:
He washed it white as snow.]

And then, brethren, there will come over the gates a Voice of sweetest music, full of the gentleness and compassion of my Savior: "Come in, thou blessed of the LORD; wherefore standest thou without?" (Genesis

24:31). And the gate will be swung wide open, and we shall have an abundant entrance into the everlasting kingdom of our Lord and Savior Jesus Christ.

Oh, He is a complete Savior. He is my Savior. My soul doth magnify the Lord. My soul shall rejoice in the Lord, brethren, tonight. Oh, I say with David, come and magnify the Lord with me, and let us exalt His name together. He has made complete satisfaction; there is not anything against us, brethren. The way is clear. The road is open. The righteousness of Christ satisfies. That is light and love and joy and eternal excellence.

Isn't it true, then, what Isaiah wrote, "Arise, shine; for thy light is come, and the glory of the LORD is risen upon thee. For, behold, the darkness shall cover the earth, and gross darkness the people: but the LORD shall arise upon thee, and his glory shall be seen upon thee" (60:1, 2). Brethren, He can do it. He wants to. Let us let Him. [Congregation: "Amen."] And let us praise Him while He is doing it.

Now, can't we praise the Lord? Then everybody in this house who wants to praise Him, you just go right ahead now. I will say amen to every word of it, for my soul magnifies Him too, brethren. My soul praises Him too because He is my Savior. He has completed the work. He has done His gracious work. He has saved me. He saves all. Let us thank Him forevermore.

CHAPTER 7

The Kingdom of God

William Miller

William Miller *(1782–1849), an avowed skeptic who served as a lieutenant and captain during the War of 1812, was converted in 1816. Continued Bible study convinced him that Jesus' second advent would take place in about 1843, and he soon felt convicted that he must share his convictions with others. His preaching, which largely consisted of a reading of the Word, appealed more to the intellect than to the emotions. Miller likely first gave this sermon Monday evening, November 14, 1842, in New York City.*

"I n the days of these kings shall the God of heaven set up a kingdom, which shall never be destroyed: and the kingdom shall not be left to other people, but it shall break in pieces and consume all these kingdoms, and it shall stand for ever" (Daniel 2:44).

Much has been said and written on this text by different commentators. Different sects and partisans have seized this text and applied it to their sect and proved, as they believe, that their sect is the true kingdom of God that will stand forever. The Catholics say it was set up in the days of the Roman Caesars, and thus claim for the pope Saint Peter's chair and the kingdom, and that the keys of this kingdom were given to the bishop of Rome at the demise of Saint Peter, and the popes have been the successors and earthly heads of this kingdom ever since.

The Baptist writers—many of them—claim a descent from the apostles for the Baptist church, making the church what the Catholics do the pope. They try to show a regular succession of the church as the Catholics do their popes. They also claim believers' baptism [immersion] as an initiatory rite into the kingdom and that none are citizens of this kingdom until they comply with this requisition.

The Episcopalians, or some of them, claim this same kingdom to have been set up in the days of the kings of England and that therefore the kings or queens of England are the accredited head of the episcopacy and rulers over the visible church. The Presbyterians say it was set up in the days of Luther among the German kings; the Quakers, in the days of Fox; the Methodists, in the days of Wesley; the Shakers, in the days of Ann Lee; and the Mormons, by Joseph Smith.

All writers seem determined to have an earthly kingdom and an earthly head to that kingdom. First Corinthians 3:3, 4 says, "Ye are yet carnal: for whereas there is among you envying, and strife, and divisions, are ye not carnal, and walk as men? For while one saith, I am of Paul; and another, I am of Apollos; are ye not carnal?" Or, as it is properly said by James, "If ye have bitter envying and strife in your hearts, glory not, and lie not against the truth. This wisdom descendeth not from above, but is earthly, sensual, devilish. For where envying and strife is, there is confusion and every evil work" (3:14–16).

Permit me to show that this kingdom is neither earthly, sensual, nor devilish. Instead, I shall show what it is, whose it is, when it is, and where it is.

What it is

The kingdom of which Daniel spoke is heavenly; for the God of heaven sets it up—that is, exalts it. It is evidently a holy kingdom; for the will of God is to be done in it as in heaven. "Thy will be done, as in heaven, so in earth" (Luke 11:2). It is a righteous kingdom. Romans 14:17, "The kingdom of God is not meat and drink; but righteousness, and peace, and joy in the Holy Ghost."

It is an everlasting kingdom—it "shall stand forever" says our text. Psalm 145:13 says, "Thy kingdom is an everlasting kingdom, and thy dominion endureth throughout all generations." Daniel 7:14 says, "There was given him dominion, and glory, and a kingdom, that all people, nations, and languages, should serve him; his dominion is an everlasting dominion, which shall not pass away, and his kingdom that which shall not be destroyed." Hebrews 12:28 says, "Wherefore we receiving a kingdom which cannot be moved, let us have grace, whereby we may serve God acceptably with reverence and godly fear." Second Peter 1:11 says, "An entrance shall be ministered unto you abundantly into the everlasting kingdom of our Lord and Saviour Jesus Christ." Revelation 11:15 says, "The seventh angel sounded; and there were great voices in heaven, saying, The kingdoms of this world are become the kingdoms of our Lord, and of his Christ; and he shall reign for ever and ever." Revelation 22:5 says, "There shall be no night there; and they need no candle, neither light of the sun; for the Lord God giveth them light: and they shall reign for ever and ever."

As there cannot be two kingdoms and both stand forever, we must naturally suppose by the tests that I have quoted that it must be a glorified kingdom. Indeed, the last text quoted proves it to be in the New

Jerusalem state—see also Psalm 24:7–10, "Lift up your heads, O ye gates; and be ye lift up, ye everlasting doors; and the King of glory shall come in. . . . Who is this King of glory? The LORD of hosts, he is the King of glory." Psalm 145:10, 11 says, "All thy works shall praise thee, O LORD; and thy saints shall bless thee. They shall speak of the glory of thy kingdom, and talk of thy power." Isaiah 2:10, 19 says, "Enter into the rock, and hide thee in the dust, for fear of the LORD, and for the glory of his majesty. . . . And they shall go into the holes of the rocks, and into the caves of the earth, for fear of the LORD, and for the glory of his majesty, when he ariseth to shake terribly the earth." Isaiah 4:2–5 says, "In that day shall the branch of the LORD be beautiful and glorious, and the fruit of the earth shall be excellent and comely for them that are escaped of Israel. And it shall come to pass, that he that is left in Zion, and he that remaineth in Jerusalem, shall be called holy, even every one that is written among the living in Jerusalem: When the Lord shall have washed away the filth of the daughters of Zion, and shall have purged the blood of Jerusalem from the midst thereof by the spirit of judgment, and by the spirit of burning. And the LORD will create upon every dwelling place of mount Zion, and upon her assemblies, a cloud and smoke by day, and the shining of a flaming fire by night: for upon all the glory shall be a defence." Isaiah 24:23 says, "The moon shall be confounded, and the sun ashamed, when the LORD of hosts shall reign in mount Zion, and in Jerusalem, and before his ancients gloriously." First Thessalonians 2:12 says, "Walk worthy of God, who hath called you unto his kingdom and glory."

If it is a glorified kingdom and an eternal kingdom, it cannot be consistent to say it is an earthly kingdom or a mortal kingdom. Christ says, "My kingdom is not of this world: if my kingdom were of this world, then would my servants fight, that I should not be delivered to the Jews: but now is my kingdom not from hence" (John 18:36). And again, in 1 Corinthians 15:50 it says, "Flesh and blood cannot inherit the kingdom of God; neither doth corruption inherit incorruption." If this be true, it cannot be in a mortal state. But I will prove it immortal. Matthew 8:11, 12 says, "Many shall come from the east and west, and shall sit down with Abraham, and Isaac, and Jacob, in the kingdom of heaven. But the children of the kingdom shall be cast out into outer darkness: there shall be weeping and gnashing of teeth." This can never be in a mortal state, for Abraham, Isaac, and Jacob, together with all the prophets, have passed from the mortal state. Then we may well conclude that the kingdom spoken of in our text is a heavenly kingdom, holy and everlasting—an eternal kingdom where its subjects will shine as the sun and all the heirs be glorified and corruption be changed into incorruption and the mortal to immortal. Then death will be swallowed up in victory.

How foolish and ridiculous the ideas that "it shall not be left to other people" if the subjects are not immortal! If deaths and births continue as now, in one hundred years death would conquer the whole kingdom and change every subject from those who received it at the beginning to their descendents. And in the fullness of time, according to the temporal millennial doctrine, the devil will be let loose and conquer a large number of children who have been literally born in the kingdom, the number of whom is as the sand of the seashore. And he will transplant them out of the eternal and everlasting kingdom of God into his kingdom and there excite them to make war against their sires in the beloved city. If our learned men can reason no better than this, I would advise them to go where they can get a little common sense before they undertake to teach people who know their right hand from the left. Were it not for the influence they obtain by newspaper puffs for which the editors make them pay well, they would obtain no more influence than their writings deserve. But let us now inquire further concerning this kingdom.

Whose it is

Whose kingdom is this one of which our text speaks? I answer, it is God's kingdom. Acts 14:22 says, "We must through much tribulation enter into the kingdom of God." Second Thessalonians 1:5 says, "Which is a manifest token of the righteous judgment of God, that ye may be counted worthy of the kingdom of God, for which ye also suffer." Both of these show that the kingdom of God was not then come, but believers were exhorted to be faithful and endure sufferings and tribulation that they might be counted worthy to obtain the kingdom of God when it should come. Therefore, none will pretend that a temporal millennium is here alluded to or that the gospel church is here meant, for these brethren were already counted worthy to belong to the church.

Again, Luke 14:15 says, "When one of them that sat at meat with him heard these things, he said unto him, Blessed is he that shall eat bread in the kingdom of God." Now, I ask, is every one blessed who eats bread in the church or in the gospel day? If so, what can the text mean that says, "Then shall ye begin to say, We have eaten and drunk in thy presence, and thou hast taught in our streets" (Luke 13:26)? Every unbiased mind must see at once that the kingdom of God of which our text speaks is not temporal, but eternal; not earthly, but heavenly.

It is a kingdom given unto Jesus Christ, the Son of man, when He leaves the mediatorial seat, gives up the redeemed church to God the Father, and the mediatorship becomes subject to God. Christ having performed all the work that the Father gave Him to do as Mediator, the mediatorial kingdom, or kingdom of grace, is given up, and the kingdom of God set up. Then Christ sits on the throne of His father David, having put down all enemies and all authority and power against His rightful reign on earth—having dashed the kingdoms to pieces like a potter's vessel, burned up the wicked, cleansed the earth, and raised the saints. Then the kingdoms of this world become the kingdoms of our Lord and of His Christ, and He shall reign forever and ever. Then Jesus will be God blessed forevermore; and His kingdom will fill the whole earth, and His tabernacle will be with men, and He will dwell with them and be their God and they shall be His people.

Now you will ask for my proof. This is right; and in my soul I wish you would be as particular with all who preach the gospel. I wish you would demand their evidences as well. Then we would have less error in our world and more truth.

First, see Daniel 7:13, 14, "I saw in the night visions, and, behold, one like the Son of man came with the clouds of heaven, and came to the Ancient of days, and they brought him near before him. And there was given him dominion, and glory, and a kingdom, that all people, nations, and languages, should serve him: his dominion is an everlasting dominion, which shall not pass away, and his kingdom that which shall not be destroyed." This proves the kingdom will be given to the Son of man.

Second, see 1 Corinthians 15:23–28, "Every man in his own order: Christ the firstfruits; afterward they that are Christ's at his coming. Then cometh the end, when he shall have delivered up the kingdom to God, even the Father; when he shall have put down all rule and all authority and power. For he must reign, till he hath put all enemies under his feet. . . . And when all things shall be subdued unto him, then shall the Son also himself be subject unto him that put all things under him, that God may be all in all."

Also, Psalm 2:9 says, "Thou shall break them with a rod of iron; thou shalt dash them in pieces like a potter's vessel." Second Peter 3:10 says, "The day of the Lord will come as a thief in the night; in the which the heavens shall pass away with a great noise, and the elements shall melt with fervent heat, the earth also and the works that are therein shall be burned up." Also, verse 13, "Nevertheless we, according to his promise, look for new heavens and a new earth, wherein dwelleth righteousness." Revelation 11:15 says, "The seventh angel sounded; and there were great voices in heaven, saying, The kingdoms of this world are become the kingdoms of our Lord, and of his Christ; and he shall reign for ever and ever."

Psalm 47:2, 7 says, "The LORD most high is terrible; he is a great King over all the earth. . . . God is the King of all the earth: sing ye praises with understanding." Zechariah 14:9 says, "The LORD shall be King over all the earth: in that day shall there be one LORD, and his name one." Romans 9:5 says, "Whose are the fathers, and of whom as concerning the flesh Christ came, who is over all, God blessed for ever. Amen." Revelation 21:3 says, "I heard a great voice out of heaven saying, Behold, the tabernacle of God is with men, and he will dwell with them, and they shall be his people, and God himself shall be with them, and be their God." These texts prove the remainder of what I have stated above.

We may further inquire, To whom is the kingdom given? I answer, it is given to the saints. See Daniel 7:21, 22, 27. "I beheld, and the same horn made war with the saints, and prevailed against them; Until the Ancient of days came, and judgment was given to the saints of the most High; and the time came that the saints possessed the kingdom. . . . And the kingdom and dominion, and the greatness of the kingdom under the whole heaven, shall be given to the people of the saints of the most High, whose kingdom is an everlasting kingdom, and all dominions shall serve and obey him." Luke 12:32 says, "Fear not, little flock; for it is your Father's good pleasure to give you the kingdom." Matthew 25:34 says, "Then shall the King say unto them on his right hand, Come, ye blessed of my Father, inherit the kingdom prepared for you from the foundation of the world." James 2:5 says, "Hath not God chosen the poor of this world rich in faith, and heirs of the kingdom which he hath promised to them that love him?" Second Peter 1:11 says, "An entrance shall be ministered unto you abundantly into the everlasting kingdom of our Lord and Savior Jesus Christ." These texts prove abundantly that the saints are to possess and inherit the everlasting kingdom of Jesus Christ.

When it is

I will now show when it is that the saints will enter this kingdom and inherit it forever. It is not in this present world, for in this world they are to suffer persecution. Also, they are strangers and pilgrims in this world. Second Timothy 3:12 says, "All that will live godly in Christ Jesus shall suffer persecution." Hebrews 11:13, 14 says, "These all died in faith, not having received the promises, but having seen them afar off, and were persuaded of them, and embraced them, and confessed that they were strangers and pilgrims on the earth. For they that say such things declare plainly that they seek a country." Also, verse 16, "They desire a better country, that is, an heavenly: wherefore God is not ashamed to be called their God: for he hath prepared for them a city."

They shall receive that kingdom at the coming of Christ with power and great glory, when He shall come in the clouds and in His kingdom. See Daniel 7:13, 14. "I saw in the night visions, and, behold, one like the Son of man came with the clouds of heaven, and came to the Ancient of days, and they brought him near before him. And there was given him dominion, and glory, and a kingdom, that all people, nations, and languages, should serve him: his dominion is an everlasting dominion, which shall not pass away, and his kingdom that which shall not be destroyed." Matthew 25:31–34 says, "When the Son of man shall come in his glory, and all the holy angels with him, then shall he sit upon the throne of his glory: And before him shall be gathered all nations: and he shall separate them one from another, as a shepherd divideth his sheep from the goats: And he shall set the sheep on his right hand, but the goats on the left. Then shall the King say unto them on his right hand, Come, ye blessed of my Father, inherit the kingdom prepared for you from the foundation of the world."

First Thessalonians 2:12 says, "That ye would walk worthy of God, who hath called you unto his kingdom and glory." First Thessalonians

3:13 says, "To the end he may stablish your hearts unblameable in holiness before God, even our Father, as at the coming of our Lord Jesus Christ with all his saints." Second Timothy 4:1 says, "I charge thee therefore before God, and the Lord Jesus Christ, who shall judge the quick and the dead at his appearing and his kingdom." Also verse 8, "Henceforth there is laid up for me a crown of righteousness, which the Lord, the righteous judge shall give me at that day: and not to me only, but unto all them also that love his appearing."

So this kingdom appears after the resurrection, for when Christ comes, He will reward His saints with His kingdom, as we have abundantly proved. Matthew 16:27 says, "The Son of man shall come in the glory of his Father, with his angels; and then he shall reward every man according to his works."

Then the kingdom of God is not yet set up?

No. But our text in Daniel 2 tells us it will be set up "in the days of those kings."

What kings?

I answer that the ten toes—of which Daniel had just been speaking—are a representation of ten kingdoms into which the iron, or fourth, kingdom should be divided. Compare Daniel 2:41, 42 with Daniel 7:23, 24. "Whereas thou sawest the feet and toes, part of potters' clay, and part of iron, the kingdom shall be divided; but there shall be in it of the strength of the iron, forasmuch as thou sawest the iron mixed with miry clay. And as the toes of the feet were part of iron, and part of clay, so the kingdom shall be partly strong, and partly broken." "Thus he said, The fourth beast shall be the fourth kingdom upon earth, which shall be diverse from all kingdoms, and shall devour the whole earth, and shall tread it down, and break it in pieces. And the ten horns out of this kingdom are ten kings that shall arise: and another shall arise after them; and he shall be diverse from the first, and he shall subdue three kings."

So, our text more than implies that these ten kings are to be in existence until Christ shall come and dash them to pieces, and they be destroyed by the brightness of His coming. Second Thessalonians 2:8 says, "Then shall that Wicked be revealed, whom the Lord shall consume with the spirit of his mouth, and shall destroy with the brightness of his coming." Also Daniel 2:45, "Forasmuch as thou sawest that the stone was cut out of the mountain without hands, and that it brake in pieces the iron, the brass, the clay, the silver, and the gold; the great God hath made known to the king what shall come to pass hereafter: and the dream is certain, and the interpretation thereof sure."

These passages are as simple and plain as words can make them. And I am bold to say that no one will or can, consistent with common sense, deny but what these ten toes do denote ten kings. I have never seen any but scoffers, skeptics, or infidels who would deny it. And if these toes do represent ten kings or kingdoms, as all good expositors do admit, there can hardly be a shadow of a doubt but we are on the very close of the kingdoms, for they have now existed more than thirteen hundred years, and this is a greater proportion than other parts of the image have borne with reference to time. And had we no other rule, we ought to bear our watchtower night and day, lest He, Christ, come and find us sleeping.

Where this kingdom is to be

I will now show where this kingdom is to be. First, it is to be under the whole heaven; see Daniel 7:2. Philippians 2:9, 10 says, "Wherefore God also hath highly exalted him, and given him a name which is above every name: That at the name of Jesus every knee should bow, of things in heaven, and things in earth, and things under the earth."

Second, it is to be on the earth. Psalm 2:8 says, "Ask of me, and I shall give thee the heathen for thine inheritance, and the uttermost parts of the earth for thy possession." Psalm 37:9 says, "Evildoers shall be cut off: but those that wait upon the LORD, they shall inherit the earth." Verse 11 says, "The meek shall inherit the earth; and shall delight themselves in the abundance of peace." Also, verse 22, "For such as be blessed of him shall inherit the earth; and they that be cursed of him shall be cut off." Isaiah 60:21 says, "Thy people also shall be all righteous: they shall inherit the land for ever, the branch of my planting, the work of my hands, that I may be glorified." Revelation 5:10 says, "And hast made us unto our God kings and priests: and we shall reign on the earth."

Third, it will be called a new earth. Isaiah 65:17 says, "Behold, I create new heavens and a new earth: and the former shall not be remembered, nor come into mind." Isaiah 66:22 says, "As the new heavens and the new earth, which I will make, shall remain before me, saith the LORD, so shall your seed and your name remain." Second Peter 3:13, "We, according to his promise, look for new heavens and a new earth, wherein dwelleth righteousness." Revelation 21:1 says, "I saw a new heaven and a new earth: for the first heaven and the first earth were passed away; and there was no more sea." Also, verse 5, "He that sat upon the throne said, Behold, I make all things new. And he said unto me, Write: for these words are true and faithful."

By the proof thus adduced, we see that the kingdom spoken of in our text is not earthly, for the kingdoms of the earth are broken to pieces and carried away and no place is found for them. This kingdom is not sensual, man ruling over man or tyrannizing over his fellow. Instead, each will do as he would have others do unto him, and each will love his neighbor as himself. It is not to be wondered at, then, that a rich man cannot easily enter this kingdom, nor one who lords it over his fellow, for the meek only can inherit it. This, too, shows why kings, captains, and mighty men are destroyed in the great battle of God Almighty— those spirits and principles cannot exist in the kingdom of God.

We learn too by this view why the earth is cleansed by fire, for the proud and all that do wickedly must be consumed out of it. See Matthew 13:41, 42. "The Son of man shall send forth his angels, and they shall gather out of his kingdom all things that offend, and them which do iniquity; And shall cast them into a furnace of fire: there shall be wailing and gnashing of teeth." This too accounts for the scoffers in these last days, for they well know that if the kingdom is to be a righteous one, they themselves can have no part in it.

We also learn by this why so many of our doctors of divinity and professors, so many of our reverends and clergy, so many of our editors and Christian teachers, as they wish to be called, are so strongly opposed to this doctrine. They know that if Christ should come, He would not pay regard to their high-sounding titles nor their dogmatical teachings. They know their great aim has been to seek honors of men and worldly profits of their dupes, and their trade is in danger. Their spiritual reign and the conversion of the world has been their hobby, and they hug to the foolish idea of converting the world to their dogmas and faith by means of money and sectarian missionaries. They might as well undertake to dip the ocean dry with a fireman's bucket as to convert the world with their sectarian motives and party creeds. How can men be so ignorant as not to see that every convert only makes the rent worse, and every year divisions and subdivisions increase? Can a kingdom thus torn and divided stand for "millions of years" as one of the sectarian editors lately proclaimed and our dear Saviour still be correct? "Jesus knew their thoughts, and said unto them, Every kingdom divided against itself is brought to desolation; and every city or house divided against itself shall not stand" (Matthew 12:25). We know they cannot be true.

Every discerning mind knows that at the present time the Roman Church is making two proselytes to the Protestants' one, and all must agree that of those converted by Protestants, one half, or nearly so, are mere nominal professors. Well may we say "millions of years" must pass away before our world could be converted. But I ask, what man of common sense who has read and believes his Bible can for a moment believe the doctrine of these foolish editors and priests who assert that "millions of years" must intervene before Christ will come? How differently did the apostle Peter preach from this: "The end of all things is at hand: be ye therefore sober, and watch unto prayer" (1 Peter 4:7). Also Christ, "Behold, I come quickly; and my reward is with me, to give every man according as his work shall be" (Revelation 22:12). And verse 20, "He which testifieth these things saith, Surely I come quickly. Amen. Even so, come, Lord Jesus." Likewise James 5:8, 9 says, "Be ye also patient; stablish your hearts: for the coming of the Lord draweth nigh. Grudge not one against another, brethren, lest ye be condemned: behold, the judge standeth before the door."

Much more Scripture might be produced to show we are on the end of the world. Scripture is being fulfilled to the very letter by these scoffers of the present day who say, "Where is the promise of His coming?" and also are "saying in their hearts, my Lord delayeth his coming." Some of them are so awfully daring as to publish openly and boldly to the world that Christ will not come this "million of years yet." Strange infatuation!

It is time for all who sincerely love our Lord to awake from their slumbers, trim their lamps, and be ready, for the Bridegroom is at the door. Why will you be so backward in believing God's Word? Can you not discern the signs of the times? I beseech you, O sinner! do not listen to these false teachers; they will deceive you. Look for yourselves. Read, study, and consider for yourselves. You may depend upon it—every important movement of the nations, of the church, of sects, and societies, and of the world denotes the end of all things is at hand. A few more days to be numbered, and time will be no more. Regard not these blasphemous hypocrites, these wicked scoffers, these false teachers who are crying peace and safety when sudden destruction cometh—these men who say, my Lord delayeth His coming. Be warned by one who feels for your souls.

I ask not for your honors, nor for your money. Let them perish with the world. I ask you to escape for your life, your eternal life. Oh! Save, save your soul! Think of that world which will never end, of that state which will never be changed. Think, my dear friend, of your own good. Buy the truth. Buy oil; buy wine and milk without money and without price.

Come, ye poor, take hold of the riches that can never perish. Eat, O eat and drink of that food which can never cloy, which if a man eat of he shall live forever. Come, ye sick, here is health for you; ye lame, you will find strength; yes, weary ones may find rest and captives will go free. The bars of the prison house will be broken, and the shackles of the slaves will be unloosed. Captain Jesus is knocking at the door. King Immanuel will soon come in!

CHAPTER 8

These Are They

Frank L. Peterson

———◆✦◆———

Frank Loris Peterson (1893–1969) attended Oakwood College, and in 1916 he became the first black man to graduate from the full four-year program at Pacific Union College. Eventually, he served as an assistant secretary of the Southern Union Conference education department, president of Oakwood College, associate secretary of the General Conference, and in 1962 he moved on to become a general vice president of the General Conference—the first black man to hold this position. Peterson preached this sermon for the Tuesday morning devotional service, July 31, 1962, at the General Conference Session held in San Francisco.

After these things I saw four angels standing on the four corners of the earth, holding the four winds of the earth, that the wind should not blow on the earth, nor on the sea, nor on any tree. And I saw another angel ascending from the east, having the seal of the living God: and he cried with a loud voice to the four angels, to whom it was given to hurt the earth and the sea, saying, Hurt not the earth, neither the sea, nor the trees, till we have sealed the servants of our God in their foreheads. And I heard the number of them which were sealed: and there were sealed an hundred and forty and four thousand of all the tribes of the children of Israel. . . .

After this I beheld, and, lo, a great multitude, which no man could number, of all nations, and kindreds, and people, and tongues, stood before the throne, and before the Lamb, clothed with white robes, and palms in their hands; and cried with a loud voice, saying, Salvation to our God which sitteth upon the throne, and unto the Lamb. . . .

And one of the elders answered, saying unto me, What are these which are arrayed in white robes? And whence came they? And I said unto him, Sir, thou knowest. And he said to me, These are they which came out of the great tribulation, and have washed their robes, and made them white in the blood of the Lamb. Therefore are they before the throne of God, and serve him day and night in his temple: and he that sitteth on the throne shall dwell among them. They shall hunger no more, neither thirst any more; neither shall the sun light on them, nor any heat. For the Lamb which is in the midst of the throne shall feed them, and shall lead them unto living fountains of waters:

98

and God shall wipe away all tears from their eyes (Revelation 7:1–4, 9, 10, 13–17).

In the book of Revelation we have the unveiling of the mysteries of the future, the greatest and most profound of which are the closing events that mark the end of the reign of sin. It is the revelation of Jesus Christ, making a people ready for His second advent; a revelation that the great controversy will soon end, and that Christ and His church will triumph.

The greatest success story in all the world is the assured climax to the preaching of the everlasting gospel. Jesus left this task with His disciples, and, as you go forth to assume the task, His assurance is, "Lo, I am with you always, even unto the end of the world" (Matthew 28:20). One of His unfailing promises is "I, if I be lifted up from the earth, will draw all men unto me" (John 12:32). Christ guarantees that if we will lift Him up, the drawing power of His love will save men.

The fact of the ultimate triumph of truth over error was established at Calvary and was verified on the morning of the Resurrection as an eternal pledge to mankind that the kingdoms of this world will become the kingdom of our Lord and of His Christ.

The sealing work

It is not my purpose here to discuss the 144,000 as such, nor the great multitude that no man could number that John saw. I do wish, however, to call your attention to the fact that they were sealed with the seal of the living God and that they were clothed with white robes and had palms in their hands. These palms are tokens of victory. The struggle with sin and Satan is over, and the victory has been won.

Whatever else may be a peculiar characteristic of the 144,000, the seal of God is not. The seal is God's character mark of obedience that is to be placed on all His children. It is a mark of exclusiveness, and either you will have it or you will not. It is the distinguishing sign of those who are God's. By this sign the Holy Spirit's power sets us aside as a "chosen generation, a royal priesthood, a holy nation, a peculiar people."

The servant of the Lord has said, "We are to be distinguished from the world because God has placed His seal upon us, because He manifests in us His own character of love. Our Redeemer covers us with His righteousness.

"In choosing men and women for His service, God does not ask whether they possess learning or eloquence or worldly wealth. He asks: 'Do they walk in such humility that I can teach them My way? Can I put My words into their lips? Will they represent Me?' "[1]

As the gospel of Jesus Christ is being preached in the world today, it is gathering out a people who will walk humbly before God and who will represent Him in the midst of this untoward generation. The gospel is now being preached to the nations of earth so that from every tongue and people Christ will raise up a new nation. He will put His words in their lips, and they will obey Him. They will be a nation clothed in His righteousness and prepared to stand in His presence. It is the everlasting gospel that will raise up a united nation on this earth. They will be the marvel of the nations. This world today has been bridged into one compact community, and the Seventh-day Adventist Church accepts the challenge this age presents. It is only the gospel that can unite men and make them one in Christ Jesus.

The work of the three angels attracted John's attention as he saw them swiftly bearing to the world the messages they were commissioned to carry. John knew that ten thousand times ten thousand of these glorified beings surrounded the throne of God to give adoration and praise to Him and to His Son. In describing this scene, John said in part,

> I saw another angel fly in the midst of heaven, having the everlasting gospel to preach unto them that dwell on the earth, and to every nation, and kindred, and tongue, and people. . . . And there followed another angel, saying, Babylon is fallen, is fallen, that great city, because she made all the nations drink of the wine of the wrath of her fornication. And the third angel followed them, saying with a loud voice, If any man worship the beast and his image, and receive his mark on his forehead, or in his hand, the same shall drink of the wine of the wrath of God, which is poured out without mixture into the cup of his indignation; and he shall be tormented with fire and brimstone in the presence of the holy angels, and in the presence of the Lamb (Revelation 14:6, 8–10).

In *The Great Controversy*, we read, "The fact that an angel is said to be the herald of this warning, is significant. By the purity, the glory, and the power of the heavenly messenger, divine wisdom has been pleased to represent the exalted character of the work to be accomplished by the message, and the power and glory that were to attend it. And the angel's flight 'in the midst of heaven,' the 'loud voice' with which the warning is uttered, and its promulgation to all 'that dwell on the earth,'—'to every nation, and kindred, and tongue, and people,'—give evidence of the rapidity and worldwide extent of the movement."[2]

Today the world stands in need of this threefold message more than it needs anything else. It is the world's best life-giving vitamin. It is God's last message to a dying world; and it is to go forth with God's power. God has designed that these messages will command the attention of the whole world and will be the means of gathering His people together.

God's other sheep

Jesus said, "Other sheep I have, which are not of this fold: them also I must bring, and they shall hear my voice; and there shall be one fold, and one shepherd" (John 10:16).

Throughout the world there are still some who will come and take their stand with the people of God who will comprise God's new nation. We have been told that "all over the world men and women are looking wistfully to heaven. Prayers and tears and inquiries go up from souls longing for light, for grace, for the Holy Spirit. Many are on the verge of the kingdom, waiting only to be gathered in."[3]

The pen of inspiration has written this assurance: "This message is the last that will ever be given to the world; and it will accomplish its work."[4] The call of God will be heard by all the honest of heart "and all the children of the Lord that remain in Babylon will heed the call, 'Come out of her, My people.' "[5] They will complete the roll of God's united nation on earth. Satan himself will yet be convinced of the powerful effect of Christ's redeeming love upon the human heart.

It is time now that we should "lay aside every weight, and the sin which doth so easily beset us, and . . . run with patience the race that is set before us" (Hebrews 12:1). All cultivated and even inherited tendencies toward sinning must be overcome. Now is the time not only to put on the whole armor of God but to keep it on.

We must get the victory over self and selfishness before we can hope to get "the victory over the beast, and over his image, and over his mark, and over the number of his name" (Revelation 15:2). "Those that over-come the world, the flesh, and the devil, will be the favored ones who shall receive the seal of the living God. Those whose hands are not clean, whose hearts are not pure, will not have the seal of the living God."[6]

We have no time to lose. The stage of the world is being set for the coming of the Lord, and little does the world know it. Rome and Prot-estantism are beginning to talk to each other. Plans are now being made for unity in church relations. We are told that within the ranks of Prot-estantism the drive toward church unity has reached colossal propor-tions. Rome is beckoning to the "brethren who strayed" to return to the fold of the mother church.

We "are all the children of light, and the children of the day: we are not of the night, nor of darkness" (1 Thessalonians 5:5). We know that the great religious agency of spiritism will unite with Protestantism, and together "they will reach over the abyss to clasp hands with the Roman power; and under the influence of this threefold union, this country will follow in the steps of Rome in trampling on the rights of conscience."[7] In that day it will take more than courage to stand up for Christ and His truth; it will take more than human reasoning. It will take the possession of "a faith that can endure weariness, delay, and hunger,—a faith that will not faint, though severely tried."[8]

Today we must be perfecting characters that would embrace such a faith. Our lives must display the result of victorious living. Whatever there is in the life that retards its spiritual growth or diminishes the soul hunger for truth and purity must be discarded. "Any habit or practice that would lead into sin, and bring dishonor upon Christ, would better be put away, whatever the sacrifice. That which dishonors God cannot benefit the soul. The blessing of heaven cannot attend any man in vio-lating the eternal principles of right. And one sin cherished is sufficient to work the degradation of the character, and to mislead others."[9]

Streets of gold

We who walk the rugged roadways and streets of this earth will one day walk on the streets of gold. John wrote, "One of the elders an-swered, saying unto me, What are these which are arrayed in white robes? and whence came they?" (Revelation 7:13). The answer is evi-dent. These are they who once lived on earth. They have long been separated by sin and by earth's confusion. Now they stand before the throne, which indicates that they are now subject to God alone. They are without fault before the throne of God because when on earth they washed their robes of character in the blood of the Lamb. They lived on earth with an awareness of God's holy presence. The atoning sacrifice of Jesus had destroyed the power of sin in their lives, and while living on earth they were on display as "symbols of what can be done for the world," and as "types of the saving power of the truths of the gospel," and "agencies in the fulfillment of God's great purpose for the human race."[10]

Among these will be many who have been gathered in this great General Conference Session, representing the many nations of earth, and for whom the atoning sacrifice of Jesus Christ has availed. These are they who have been made captives by the preaching of the everlasting gospel and whose lives have been purified and made white. Whatever may have been their lot as Christians on earth, they found in service to God their deepest satisfaction.

"The great controversy between truth and error, between Christ and Satan, is to increase in intensity to the close of this world's history."[11] "The remnant church will then be brought into great trial and distress. Those who keep the commandments of God and the faith of Jesus, will feel the ire of the dragon and his hosts. Satan numbers the world as his subjects; he has gained control even of many professing Christians. But here is a little company who are resisting his supremacy. If he could blot them from the earth, his triumph would be complete."[12]

As we draw near the end of time and enter into this final conflict, God's people in all lands must press together. We must stand solidly against the enemy. We must allow no divisions to creep in among us—whether they be national, racial, or doctrinal—that it may be said of us, that these are they who stand in defense of the gospel and who are seeking the heavenly inheritance.

---

1. Ellen G. White, *Testimonies for the Church* (Mountain View, Calif.: Pacific Press®, 1948), 7:144.

2. White, *The Great Controversy* (Mountain View, Calif.: Pacific Press®, 1950), 355.

3. White, *The Acts of the Apostles* (Mountain View, Calif.: Pacific Press®, 1911), 109.

4. White, *The Great Controversy*, 390.

5. Ibid.

6. White, *Testimonies to Ministers and Gospel Workers* (Mountain View, Calif.: Pacific Press®, 1944), 445.

7. White, *The Great Controversy*, 588.

8. Ibid., 621.

9. White, *The Desire of Ages* (Mountain View, Calif.: Pacific Press®, 1940), 439.

10. White, *Testimonies,* 6:11.

11. White, *The Great Controversy*, 144.

12. White, *Prophets and Kings* (Mountain View, Calif.: Pacific Press®, 1943), 587.

CHAPTER 9

The Second Advent: The Keynote of the Message

W. W. Prescott

———————◆———————

William Warren Prescott (1855–1944) accepted the position of president of Battle Creek College in 1885. He helped found Union College in 1891 and became its first president, and the next year assumed the presidency of the newly founded Walla Walla College as well—presiding over all three colleges simultaneously! Later he taught at Bible institutes, strengthened the church's educational interests around the world, served as editor of the Review and Herald, *held various administrative positions in the General Conference, and worked as a college Bible teacher. Prescott preached this sermon as the morning Bible study on Wednesday, June 2, 1926, at the General Conference Session held in Milwaukee, Wisconsin.*

I saw another angel fly in the midst of heaven, having the everlasting gospel to preach unto them that dwell on the earth, and to every nation, and kindred, and tongue, and people, saying with a loud voice, Fear God, and give glory to him; for the hour of his judgment is come: and worship him that made heaven, and earth, and the sea, and the fountains of waters. . . . And I looked, and behold a white cloud, and upon the cloud one sat like unto the Son of man, having on his head a golden crown, and in his hand a sharp sickle" (Revelation 14:6–14).

In this outline of the everlasting gospel message for this time, three things stand out with clearness. The return of Christ to our world will not be long delayed—let this be the keynote of every message. And in the message of preparation, two things that stand out clearly are the mediatorial work of Christ as our High Priest in the heavenly sanctuary at a time when the hour of His judgment is come, when He enters upon a new phase of His mediatorial work—the cleansing of the sanctuary on the great Day of Atonement. Along with this, the Sabbath of the Lord is suggested in the words "worship Him that made." These two great truths, represented by the sanctuary and the Sabbath, have marked this movement from its beginning and should mark it to the close. Now, we ought to see more clearly what is involved in these two things, the mediatorial work of Christ and the Sabbath.

The central Person in the gospel is Jesus Christ, Son of God and Son of man, our Savior and our Mediator. The central principle in the gospel is the mediatorial work. And the Sabbath is the sign of the work of God in the original creation and in the new creation, and therefore becomes the sign of the gospel, the sign of the covenant of grace and redemption. As such, it must take its place in connection with the mediatorial work of Christ, who is the mediator of the new covenant.

When we come to the final message, we find these two things joined again in this movement. And when we survey the history of God's people from of old, we find that their relation to the sanctuary service and their recognition of the meaning of the Sabbath as the sign of sanctification has marked their experience. When they lost the meaning of the sanctuary and the Sabbath, they lost their relationship with God—they apostatized from Him. And when they returned, it was through messages calling for the restoration of the true worship of God in the sanctuary in the spiritual sense and the recognition of the Sabbath in its spiritual meaning, as the sign of the gospel of Christ, the Mediator.

For example, we find the prophet Ezekiel telling the people the reason for the captivity. He said it was because they defiled the sanctuary and profaned the Sabbath (Ezekiel 23:38). Coming down to the time of Christ, we find these same two gospel truths neglected, overlaid with tradition. Central in Christ's teaching was His restoration of the Sabbath to its true place and His cleansing of the sanctuary. We find Him saying to the religious leaders, "My house shall be called a house of prayer: but ye make it a den of robbers" (Matthew 21:13, ASV). We find Him saying to the men who had overlaid the Sabbath truth with their tradition until it was a burdensome things, "It is lawful to do good on the Sabbath day," restoring the true spiritual meaning of Sabbath keeping.

We will observe that at that time there were two Sabbaths. There was indeed a Jewish sabbath at that time—a man-made sabbath, a sabbath to be observed according to human regulations. It is true that it came upon the seventh day of the week, but it was not the Lord's Sabbath. Christ did not observe the Jewish sabbath, and they charged Him with being a sinner because He broke the sabbath day. He restored to them the true Sabbath of the Lord in place of their sabbath of tradition.

The great apostasy

You pass on into history, and you come to the time of the great apostasy—that great apostasy prophesied of by the apostle Paul when, speaking of Christ's coming, he said, "That day shall not come, except there come a falling away first [the apostasy], and that man of sin be revealed, the son of perdition; who opposeth and exalteth himself above all that is called God, or that is worshipped; so that he as God sitteth in the temple of God, shewing himself [setting himself forth] that he is God" (2 Thessalonians 2:3, 4; compare Daniel 7:25).

What two things marked the apostasy of the Dark Ages so clearly? The substitution of man-made service in place of the true mediatorial service, a sanctuary upon earth instead of a sanctuary in heaven, a human priest instead of the Priest who is the Son of God, a human offering in place of the divine offering—a complete counterfeit. Of course there must come with that false mediatorial service the false sabbath because they are joined together in such a way that they cannot be separated. They are mentioned together in the Scriptures, and when they are found in history, they are found together: the perverted sanctuary service and the false sabbath. We have a false mediator in place of the true Mediator, and a false sabbath as the sign, or mark, of his authority.

When we understand clearly the significance of the Sabbath of the Lord, when that is brought before us in the spiritual meaning, and we see the place that God has given to it in the gospel of grace and salvation, we shall see more clearly than ever what a horrible thing is the mark of the beast. Then we shall warn people against it, and we shall make it more clear to them what a desirable thing it is to shun the mark of the beast as we make clear to them what God's mark, or sign, or seal, really means.

Now, we observe that in restoration eras that have followed times of apostasy, the Sabbath and the sanctuary have been emphasized. Go back to the Babylonian captivity. The prophet Ezekiel told the Israelites they had been taken captive because they had defiled the sanctuary of God and had profaned His Sabbath. When the restoration came after the expiration of the seventy years of captivity and the prophets Haggai and Zechariah led the people in their work, what was the message? They were to go up to the mountain and get wood and build the house of Jehovah. In other words, they were to restore the sanctuary and its service—to restore the worship of Jehovah in the temple as He had appointed it.

Read the book of Nehemiah, supplementing the history given us in the book of Ezra, and you will note what he added to the message given by Ezra: "There dwelt men of Tyre also therein, who brought fish, and all manner of ware, and sold on the sabbath unto the children of Judah, and in Jerusalem. Then I contended with the nobles of Judah, and said unto them, What evil thing is this that ye do, and profane the sabbath day? Did not your fathers thus, and did not our God bring all this evil upon us, and upon this city? yet ye bring more wrath upon Israel by profaning the sabbath" (Nehemiah 13:16–18).

What does he say was the real root cause of the Babylonian captivity? It was profaning the Sabbath, joined with defiling the sanctuary. When the restoration era came, the sanctuary and its service must be restored, and the Sabbath must be restored.

So it was in the Reformation that Christ wrought concerning these two leading features of the gospel, the reformation to restore true worship. How did He do it? The time had come when all that typical service was to be taken away. Through the descent of the Holy Spirit, Christ brought to them the knowledge of the heavenly sanctuary, the heavenly truths, the heavenly service, and what that meant in the Christian life and experience. He restored to them the true meaning of the Sabbath.

Then the apostasy came, as we have said. The Sabbath and the sanctuary were both perverted. And what do we find in history as soon as those great prophetic periods, the 1,260 years, the 1,290 years, the 1,335 years, the 2,300 years, had expired, bringing us down to the year 1844? We find that exactly at that time there arose this Second Advent movement. And the light that set this movement upon the right road after the Great Disappointment of 1844 was the light concerning the Sabbath and the sanctuary. Even though they were so bitterly disappointed on the twenty-second day of October 1844, yet they had such a personal experience with their Lord that they knew the message was true. They could not give it up, so they waited for additional light. That light came. It was the light upon the Sabbath and the sanctuary. This movement is founded upon those great truths, and it must stay upon that foundation.

Let me ask you in all frankness, Has there not been a tendency to let these three things become more or less subordinate in our preaching?

"Ah! But," you say, "isn't this message the message of righteousness by faith?"

Yes, it is. But in this message you cannot separate righteousness by faith from the sanctuary and the Sabbath and have the true message. [Many Amens.]

Isn't this the message of reform in all lines of Christian living and working?

Yes it is. But the key to it all, and the foundation of it all, is found right here. And when we neglect the keynote of our message, and when we let fall into the background the Sabbath and the sanctuary, we shall lose the power of this message.

Not sanctuary and Sabbath alone

The point isn't that I am to say only, "Sanctuary—Sabbath; sanctuary—Sabbath; sanctuary—Sabbath." It means that I am to find out from the Scriptures what those words comprehend. The whole Bible belongs to this movement. This is the final and the broadest preaching of the gospel that can ever be given. To narrow it down to a few texts, to a kind of a shibboleth, is to lose it. But mark you this, wherever you draw your material, from Genesis to Revelation, it must be molded by the spirit of this message given to us in the fourteenth chapter of Revelation in order that it may be the preaching of the gospel that belongs to this time.

Justification by faith—Luther preached it. But we are not to preach justification by faith just as Luther preached it. We have entered upon a new era. All truth has taken on a new mold—a new, fuller meaning, as it were. Since the prophetic periods have expired, our Mediator has entered upon a new phase of His work. Christ is now doing something that He was not doing previous to 1844, and we must know what He is doing and cooperate with Him in what He is doing in order to give the gospel message that belongs to this time.

Notice how earnestly attention was called to the question of the Sabbath when this movement arose: "In the ark was the golden pot of manna, Aaron's rod that budded, and the tables of stone, which folded together like a book. Jesus opened them, and I saw the ten commandments written on them with the finger of God. On one table were four, on the other six. The four on the first table shone brighter than the other six. But the fourth, the Sabbath commandment, shone above them all; for the Sabbath was set apart to be kept in honor of God's holy name. The holy Sabbath looked glorious—a halo of glory was all around it. I saw that the Sabbath commandment was not nailed to the cross."[1]

Again, *The Great Controversy:* "The Sabbath will be the great test of loyalty; for it is the point of truth especially controverted. When the final test shall be brought to bear upon men, then the line of distinction will be drawn between those who serve God and those who serve Him not."[2]

Thus was the Sabbath emphasized at the very beginning of this movement in the same way the sanctuary was emphasized. It was because of the light that came to this people concerning these two fundamental truths that this advent movement was set on the right way, and it will emphasize those truths as long as it keeps on that right way.

Now mark again the development of the gospel in the work of Christ. His incarnation, His sinless life, His atoning death, His resurrection, His ascension, His entering upon His priestly work are so many steps, all absolutely necessary, and yet only steps toward this one thing, the goal of His redemptive work. "Christ hath redeemed us from the curse of the law, being made a curse for us: . . . that we might receive the promise of the Spirit through faith" (Galatians 3:13, 14). The gift of the Holy Spirit, the Comforter, was the goal of Christ's redemptive work. All these other things were absolutely necessary, but they all tended toward this one thing. Hear Christ's own statement: "Now on the last day, the great day of the feast, Jesus stood and cried, saying, If any man thirst, let him come unto me and drink. He that believeth on me, as the scripture hath said, from within him shall flow rivers of living water. But this spake he of the Spirit, which they that believed on him were to receive: for the Spirit was not yet given; because Jesus was not yet glorified" (John 7:37–39, ASV).

The glorification of Christ

The glorification of Christ was essential to the outpouring of the Spirit. And what was that glorification? "The hour is come, that the Son of man should be glorified. . . . Except a grain of wheat fall into the earth and die, it abideth by itself alone; but if it die, it beareth much fruit" (John 12:23, 24, ASV). The glorification of Jesus was His triumphant death, resurrection, ascension, and His crowning. Hear it:

> Christ's ascension to heaven was the signal that His followers were to receive the promised blessing. . . . When Christ passed within the heavenly gates, He was enthroned amidst the adoration of the angels. As soon as this ceremony was completed, the Holy Spirit descended upon the disciples in rich currents, and

Christ was indeed glorified, even with the glory which He had with the Father from all eternity. The Pentecostal outpouring was Heaven's communication that the Redeemer's inauguration was accomplished. According to His promise, He had sent the Holy Spirit from heaven to His followers, as a token that He had, as priest and king, received all authority in heaven and on earth, and was the Anointed One over His people.[3]

Now mark the Scripture. On the Day of Pentecost, Peter declared to his audience the facts of Christ's death, His resurrection, and His ascension. Then he said of Christ that "being therefore by the right hand of God exalted, and having received of the Father the promise of the Holy Spirit, he hath poured forth this, which ye see and hear" (Acts 2:33, ASV).

The outpouring of the Holy Spirit directly referred to the entrance of Christ upon His work as high priest in the heavenly sanctuary. But He entered upon His work in the holy place. That was the early rain. Now we follow Him in His mediatorial work in harmony with the type, and when we come to the great Day of Atonement, when we come to the time for the cleansing of the sanctuary and our High Priest changes His ministry from the Holy Place to the Most Holy Place, a new era is inaugurated, a new power in greater fullness is provided. We cannot and must not attempt to separate the pouring out of the Spirit in the latter rain from the priestly work of Christ as He begins cleansing the heavenly sanctuary.

The cleansing of the sanctuary in heaven is not something apart from the work here upon earth. "We are a temple of the living God; even as God said, I will dwell in them, and walk in them." "Know ye not that your body is a temple of the Holy Spirit which is in you, which ye have from God?" (2 Corinthians 6:16, ASV; 1 Corinthians 6:19, ASV). There is such a connection between the temple in heaven and His temple on earth—believers, the church—that the cleansing of the sanctuary in heaven means the cleansing of the sanctuary upon earth. It means the mighty power of the Holy Spirit in His fullness to remove all sin and to bring out a company of Sabbath keepers.

What does Sabbath keeping mean? Of what is it a sign? It is not a form. It is not a ceremony. It is not something merely outward. It is a sign of an inward experience—the inward experience set before us in

Hebrews 4:10, "He that is entered into his rest hath himself also rested from his works, as God did from his" (ASV).

Man's works as man's works are always sinful. "I know that in me (that is, in my flesh,) dwelleth no good thing." All that any individual can do of himself is vitiated, polluted with sin. To enter into Christ's rest is to cease from sin; and the Sabbath is the sign of that power which will lift us above the power of sin and save us from sinning. The last movement must have that power of the gospel, that personal indwelling of the Christ, that shall keep us from sinning.

It is no use for us to talk about a mere dogma, a mere theory. We face this proposition: Am I willing to have my sins taken away absolutely? What does such willingness involve? More than assent to a creed. More than saying Amen loudly in a meeting. It means an absolutely different order of living.

See what we are surrounded with. See how rampant sin is. See how it is flaunted in your face every time you walk the streets—a low grade of morals, a spirit of frivolity and foolishness, the spirit of the world. Is it shut out from our lives? Are we really Sabbath keepers? Have we really laid hold upon that power which our High Priest ministers from the heavenly sanctuary to save us from all that is of the world and the spirit of the world and to bring us into personal fellowship and union with Jesus Christ? That is what this message means. Are we witnessing to this message not simply in words but in life? And does that power attend our message, marking it as a message for this time—the message to meet the world's need?

In simple terms

I am always asking, Now tell me how. Come right down to the simple thing, and tell me how about it. Don't use mere theological phrases; just talk with me as you would talk to a person, and tell me how it is.

So, if I sat down by your side to try to tell you how, I think I would say something like this: Christ was here in a body, and He did a work in His own body. He has now returned to heaven, having been glorified through His death, resurrection, and ascension, and has taken His place as the Anointed One over His people. It is now His privilege and His joy to minister to our need.

Our greatest need is the gift of Himself in the person of the Holy Spirit, the Comforter. Christ was born of the Spirit. He was anointed at His baptism with the Spirit. He was filled with the Spirit. He returned from His temptation in the power of the Spirit. He wrought all His wonderful works by the Spirit. So He said, "If I by the Spirit of God cast out demons, then is the kingdom of God come upon you" (Matthew 12:28, ASV).

The union between us and Jesus Christ is not a union of flesh with flesh but a union of spirit with Spirit. "Now the Lord is the Spirit" (2 Corinthians 3:17, ASV). "He that is joined unto the Lord is one spirit" (1 Corinthians 6:17). So what we know of Christ now—the present Christ, the working Christ—is Christ in the Spirit. His Spirit witnesses with our spirit; and His Spirit—taking possession of our spirit, ruling our spirit, through our spirit revealing Himself, His life, His power—transforms us and makes us Christians. And He does this without interfering with our individuality and without destroying our personality. You do not become me, and I do not become you. We are all members of the one body, partakers of the one Spirit, even the Spirit of the God-man—broad enough, so to speak, to recognize the individuality of every person and to work through him as he is and transform him into the righteousness of Christ. Yet that Spirit does not interfere with the individual's will, his personality, his individuality.

It all depends on our willingness for this to be done. "If we consent, He will so identify Himself with our thoughts and aims, so blend our hearts and minds into conformity to His will, that when obeying Him we shall be but carrying out our own impulses."[4]

Notice! "If we consent, He will so identify Himself with our thoughts . . ." He cannot identify Himself with our thoughts when we are thinking all sorts of foolishness and frivolity. I know the devil can put evil thoughts into our minds, but he cannot keep them there unless we consent. It is not a sin to be tempted. It is not a sin to have an evil thought thrust into the mind. It is in harboring that evil thought that we commit sin.

What is the remedy? His thoughts are not as our thoughts. Fill the mind with His thoughts. Think His thoughts after Him. Fill the mind with the Word of God. When the devil talks to you, talk back in the language of the Scripture, and he will flee. I know it. That is my idea of the Christian life, of Christian living. "Christ in you, the hope of glory"

(Colossians 1:27). "Strengthened with might by his Spirit in the inner man; that Christ may dwell in your hearts by faith" (Ephesians 3:16, 17). "Hereby know we that we dwell in him, and he in us, because he hath given us of his Spirit" (1 John 4:13). Here is the secret of the restoration of fellowship with Him.

> The message that we have to bear is not one that we need cringe to declare. Its advocates are not to seek to cover it, to conceal its origin and purpose. As those who have made solemn vows to God, and who have been commissioned as the messengers of Christ, as stewards of the mysteries of grace, we are under obligation to declare faithfully the whole counsel of God.
>
> We are not to make less prominent the special truths that have separated us from the world, and made us what we are; for they are fraught with eternal interests. God has given us light in regard to the things that are now taking place, and with pen and voice we are to proclaim the truth to the world. But it is the life of Christ in the soul, it is the active principle of love imparted by the Holy Spirit, that alone will make our words fruitful. The love of Christ is the force and power of every message for God that ever fell from human lips.[5]

In this message there is a truth that is not found anywhere else. Light has come to us in this movement that has not come to others, and it is light with reference to what Christ is doing now. It is important that we should know what He is doing now in order that we may cooperate with Him, as always we must if we are God's fellow workers.

> The great plan of redemption, as revealed in the closing work for these last days, should receive close examination. The scenes connected with the sanctuary above should make such an impression upon the minds and hearts of all that they may be able to impress others. All need to become more intelligent in regard to the work of the atonement, which is going on in the sanctuary above. When this grand truth is seen and understood, those who hold it will work in harmony with Christ to prepare a people to stand in the great day of God, and their efforts will be successful. By study, contemplation, and prayer, God's people

will be elevated above common, earthly thoughts and feelings, and will be brought into harmony with Christ and His great work of cleansing the sanctuary above from the sins of the people. Their faith will go with Him into the sanctuary.[6]

Any one who lives in that atmosphere, who joins in spirit with our High Priest in the work He is doing now, will be lifted above the cheap, the common, the frivolous, the earthly. He will be filled with a sense of heavenly things, and, like Enoch of old, while still living on the earth, will live in the atmosphere of heaven. That is the experience that belongs to every true Seventh-day Adventist, and that is the experience to which we invite people.

Everyone who preaches Christ today as Christ must be preached in order to give the gospel message due at this time will produce Seventh-day Adventists! Why? Because they are the people of the time, the people of the hour. And because this message—finding the keynote in the return of Christ—declares the great truths of the gospel for this time in the mediatorial work of Christ in the sanctuary and in this Sabbath as the sign of our sanctification.

Cling to the fundamental truths of this message!

---

1. Ellen G. White, *Early Writings* (Washington, D.C.: Review and Herald®, 1945), 32, 33.

2. White, *The Great Controversy* (Mountain View, Calif.: Pacific Press®, 1950), 605.

3. White, *The Acts of the Apostles* (Mountain View, Calif.: Pacific Press®, 1911), 38, 39.

4. White, *The Desire of Ages* (Mountain View, Calif.: Pacific Press®, 1940), 668.

5. White, *Gospel Workers* (Washington, D.C.: Review and Herald®, 1948), 288.

6. White, *Testimonies for the Church* (Mountain View, Calif.: Pacific Press®, 1948), 5:575.

CHAPTER 10

Can Man Bridge the River of Death?

J. L. Shuler

John L. Shuler *(1887–1984) spent seventy some years in the ministry of the Seventh-day Adventist Church, primarily as an evangelist. He introduced many innovations to Adventist evangelism and wrote numerous articles and books as well. He was active nearly to the end of his life, reading the edited galleys of his last book just weeks before his death at the age of ninety-seven. This sermon was published in 1940 in a sampler of Adventist evangelistic sermons titled* Typical Evangelistic Sermons.

In one of our large eastern cities, a four-story frame apartment house in a poorer section of the city caught fire. Trapped on the top floor were a father and three boys, aged three, five, and seven. The stairways were a mass of flame and smoke. There seemed to be no way of escape. It looked as if all were doomed to a horrible death—to be burned alive. The father ran to a window on the side of the building. There was an open space of a little more than three feet between the burning building and the adjoining structure and an open window right across from the window he was looking through.

The desperate father saw that if he would stretch himself across the intervening space and grasp the sill of the open window, his boys could crawl over his body into the adjacent building and be saved. He immediately called the three boys and told them to climb quickly over the bridge he would form with his body between these two buildings. The last little lad had just climbed over his father's body and reached the opposite apartment house in safety when the father's strength failed, and he fell to the ground and was killed.

Life is a journey from the cradle to the grave. Eventually, every soul must come to the brink of the river of death. When you do, you will want to find a bridge on which you can cross into a better world. Science, education, philosophy, reason, and culture have all made valuable contributions to life in this world, but none of them can give you any help on that day. Let us thank God that by the revelation of the gospel of Jesus Christ, He has provided a way whereby we may pass from death to life. The best news that you have ever heard is contained in one of the 31,173 verses that comprise the sixty-six books of Holy Scripture—John 3:16, that wonderful love verse— "God so loved the world, that he gave his only begotten Son, that whosoever believeth in him should not perish, but have everlasting life."

On a night long ago a lonely wanderer in Judea laid himself down upon the ground to sleep with a stone for his pillow. As he gazed at the twinkling orbs above his bed, doubtless the same questions came into his mind that have occurred to many other men. How far is it beyond those stars to where God reigns on the throne of the universe? Is God really taking note of me and my situation? Is it possible for me to ascend to these stars and on to God's great home?

God answered Jacob's questions that night in a wonderful dream. He saw a bright, shining ladder, the base of which rested upon the ground at his feet, while the topmost round reached to heaven, unto the very throne of God. On this ladder, angels of God were ascending and descending. This was a divine assurance that the great gulf between sinful man and a holy God has been bridged so that man can commune with God and someday can actually ascend into heaven to dwell with God.

That bright, shining ladder reaching from earth to heaven is a symbol of Jesus Christ, Son of man and Son of God. When Jesus called Nathanael to follow Him, He told him, "Hereafter ye shall see heaven open, and the angels of God ascending and descending upon the Son of man" (John 1:51). Christ is the way—the only way—whereby anyone can ever go to heaven.

The great gospel bridge

The great gospel bridge spans the fearful gulf from man lost in sin to man saved forever in the kingdom of God. Seven piers sustain this bridge—the gospel resolves itself into a sevenfold view of the work and office of Jesus Christ by which He can take sinners from this present evil world and transport them over the river of sin and death into that better world of the future.

On the first pier of this gospel bridge is inscribed the word "Incarnation." By incarnation we mean the entrance of the Son of God into human flesh in order to save man. This act made possible that wondrous news that you have heard repeated so often at the Christmas season: "The angel said unto them, Fear not: for, behold, I bring you good tidings of great joy, which shall be to all people. For unto you is born this day in the city of David a Saviour, which is Christ the Lord" (Luke 2:11).

It is plain that in order for Christ to provide a way whereby man, lost in sin, could come to God, that figurative ladder must reach all the way to the throne of God. Our Savior, then, must be divine. If Jesus Christ weren't divine as God the Son, then the ladder wouldn't reach to the throne of God, and we would be left without hope and forever lost.

On the other hand, if the ladder failed by a single step of reaching the earth, we would be irreparably lost because we couldn't reach the ladder to heaven. The Savior must be human as well as divine. The Son of God must become the Son of man that the sons of men may through Him become the sons of God. In Christ alone, as the God-man—the Son of God and the Son of man—we have a complete, all-sufficient Savior.

Think of the immeasurable love of God that the provision of this incarnation represents. In order to save you, the Father so loved you that He gave the best gift of heaven for you. The Son, in turn, so loved you that He willingly and gladly left His exalted and infinitely happy place at the Father's side and was born here as a child of the human family. O how we ought to thank Jesus anew each day that He was willing to give up His high and happy station in heaven and come to this sinful world to save us. How dark would be our future, how utterly hopeless our lot, if He hadn't come to earth nineteen centuries ago!

Many Christians have missed or lost the real Christ of the Bible because they think of Him as existing only from the time of His birth in Bethlehem. Anyone who considers Christ as existing only from His birth by the virgin Mary has missed the true Christ of the Scriptures and the real Savior of men.

Did Christ exist before His birth at Bethlehem? Hear His own words in that wonderful prayer of John 17. He said, "Now, O Father, glorify Thou Me with Thine own Self with the glory which I had with Thee before the world was" (paraphrase). He who as a babe was laid in the manger at Bethlehem had been with the Father before the world existed. One of the outstanding revelations of the New Testament is that the Jesus of Bethlehem and the Christ of Nazareth is the Creator of our world. Thus we read in John 1:1–3: "In the beginning was the Word, and the Word was with God, and the Word was God. . . . All things were made by him."

Who is this Word by whom all things were made in the beginning? Verse 14 explains that this Word is Christ: "The Word was made flesh, and dwelt among us." John 1:1, 2 may be paraphrased in these words: "In the beginning was Christ, and Christ was with God the Father, and Christ was God the Son. . . . All things were made by Christ."

Micah 5:2, the very prophecy that foretold that the Christ would be born in Bethlehem, declared that this wonderful babe of Bethlehem is He whose goings forth are from the days of eternity. Note that Jesus Christ is not merely from Bethlehem but also from the days of eternity. A new being was not brought into existence when the virgin Mary conceived and brought forth a child named Jesus. Rather, a change was made in the person of the eternal Son of God. He who had been with the Father and was in His form and likeness from the days of eternity took upon Himself the form and likeness of a man to dwell with men. By His incarnation—by His coming to this world and entering human flesh—Jesus Christ began to build the bridge across that fearful gulf between man lost and dying in sin and man living eternally with God.

A sinless life

In order to save us, Christ must live a sinless life in the flesh. So, the second pier under this great gospel bridge of salvation is labeled "Sinless Life."

If Christ had committed even just one sin, we would be without hope today. The Bible says, "Sin is the transgression of the law." If Christ had broken the Ten Commandments, He would have become a sinner and He could not have been our Savior. If He had transgressed any one of the Ten Commandments, if He had yielded to sin just once, He would have immediately come under the condemnation of the law and could not have redeemed us from its curse.

He was tempted in all points like we are yet was without sin. Where the first Adam failed, the Second Adam succeeded. He didn't sin. This second support under the bridge over the river of sin and death stands secure forever. Christ lived a sinless life. O how we ought to love Him and be true to Him who stood every test for us! Aren't you glad He did?

By living a sinless life from the time of His birth, Jesus extended this great bridge a bit farther across the chasm between our lost condition and eternal life on that better shore. But the bridge must be extended till it actually reaches the golden strand on the farther side if it is to bridge the river of death into the better world. In order to save us, Christ must not only enter human flesh—the Incarnation—and live a sinless life, but He must die for our sins. This brings us to the third pier, which is labeled "Crucifixion." The death of Christ for our sins is the central feature, the very heart, of the gospel.

Sometimes people ask, "If Christ were the Savior of men when He was born, why then did He have to die to save man? Why couldn't He have accomplished our salvation without dying?" The answer is that in order to save us, Christ had to pay the penalty for our transgressions of the law of God. First John 3:4 says, "Sin is the transgression of the law," and God's decree is, "The soul that sinneth, it shall die."

The law of God condemns every soul in the world to death because everyone has transgressed God's commandments. "All have sinned." But Christ loves you so much that He says, "I can't bear to see you perish. I'll die in your place. I'll take on Myself that deathblow that the law has aimed at you. I will go to the cross for you." Does not His giving His own precious life to save you cause you to love Him? Since He gave Himself for you, aren't you ready now to give yourself to Him—to live for Him who died for you?

On account of transgression of the law, the human race passed under the death sentence. This tremendous crisis could be dealt with in just one of three ways: (1) by letting man die for his own transgression, (2) by abolishing the law and thus canceling the penalty, or (3) by a divine Substitute taking man's guilt and dying in his stead.

God couldn't cancel the penalty by abolishing His law because that would have made His government a failure. But God so loved the world that He wouldn't let man die to pay the penalty for his violation of the divine law. Since the law of God is as sacred as God Himself, only one equal with God could make atonement for men's transgression of it. In all the universe there was but One who could, in behalf of man, satisfy its claims. None but Christ, the Father's only begotten Son, could redeem fallen man from the curse of the law and bring him again into harmony with heaven.

Love, and love alone, provided a way whereby man could be saved. The Father gave His own dear Son to be man's Savior, and the Son gave His own life on the cross to make our salvation possible. I don't believe that anyone can behold Jesus Christ dying on the cross in his stead and still withhold himself from such a loving Savior.

Were the whole realm of nature mine,
That were a tribute far too small;
Love so amazing, so divine,
Demands my life, my soul, my all.

When I consider that He gave Himself for me, what else can I do but give myself to Him? Would it not be the basest ingratitude for me to refuse or neglect to live for Him who died for me?

The fourth pier

By His vicarious death on Calvary, Jesus provided another essential section in this bridge from death to life. But His death didn't make salvation complete. After He died for us, He had to rise again from the dead. This brings us to the fourth pier, on which is inscribed the word "Resurrection."

If Jesus Christ had never risen from the dead, we would still have been eternally lost in spite of His incarnation, His sinless life, and His crucifixion. Paul says, "If Christ be not raised, your faith is vain; ye are yet in your sins" (1 Corinthians 15:17). A dead Savior couldn't save anybody. But let us thank God that He who died for us also rose again. We sing of a Christ who is "not in the tomb where once He lay" but is a risen Christ who is alive forevermore. Death couldn't hold Him. On the third day He burst asunder the bands of the tomb and walked forth as a mighty conqueror over death and the grave.

By His resurrection Jesus erected another section of this great bridge of salvation over the river of death and destruction. But more is needed yet to make the bridge reach to that blissful shore of the better world to come. Christ must not only rise from the dead, but He must also ascend to heaven. He who came from God must go back to God to open the way for us to go to God. This brings us to pier number five, labeled "Ascension." Forty days after His resurrection He ascended up on high. As Paul says in Ephesians 4:10, "He that descended is the same also that ascended up far above all heavens, that he might fill all things."

By His ascension to heaven Jesus erected another section of this bridge from death to life. But His ascension was only prefatory to another essential step in the plan of salvation. As our Savior He must perform a certain work for us in heaven after His ascension. Thus you will note that the gospel bridge has a sixth support, labeled "Mediation."

Christ ascended to heaven to sit on the right hand of God as our Mediator, High Priest, and Intercessor to plead the merits of His shed blood for all who accept Him as their Savior. In 1 John 2:1 we read, "If any man sin, we have an advocate with the Father, Jesus Christ the righteous." And Paul tells us in Hebrews 7:25 that Christ is "able also to save them to the uttermost that come unto God by him, seeing he ever liveth to make intercession for them."

Christ is able to save to the uttermost all who will come to Him. If you will do the coming, Christ will do the saving. If you will step out to accept Him, He will meet you with pardon, peace, and salvation. If you will give yourself to Him for a closer walk with Him, to live a better life for Him, He will provide you with power to live that better life. If you will confess your sins to Him in repentance and faith, He will raise those nail-pierced hands to plead for you. He will cry, "My blood! My blood!! My blood!!! Father, I shed My blood for that soul who accepts Me, and I claim pardon for him at Thy hand." Aren't you ready to put your case in His hands this very day by yielding yourself to Him?

By His priestly mediation Jesus extended this bridge a bit farther, until it lacks only one more section of reaching that golden strand where the called, the chosen, and the faithful will be with Christ forever. Christ must not only plead for us as Mediator but He must come again to take His people to Himself. This is according to His own blessed promise: "Let not your heart be troubled: ye believe in God, believe also in me. In my Father's house are many mansions: if it were not so, I would have told you. I go to prepare a place for you. And if I go and prepare a place for you, I will come again, and receive you unto myself; that where I am, there ye may be also" (John 14:1–3).

This brings us to the seventh pier, which supports the final section of the gospel bridge. This is labeled "Second Advent," which is the consummating event in the plan of redemption. The second coming of Christ is just as necessary in God's plan of eternal redemption as is the Crucifixion or the Resurrection. Thus Paul tells us, "Christ was once offered to bear the sins of many; and unto them that look for him shall he appear the second time without sin unto salvation" (Hebrews 9:28). By His second advent Jesus provides the section of that bridge that will actually land His faithful ones on that shore where the billows cease to roll, where sorrow, trouble, and death will be no more.

Seven essentials

The bridge is now complete, ready for you to cross the gulf from "lost in sin" to "eternal life in the kingdom of God." Are you ready to accept it point by point and cross over the gulf?

In order to save you, Christ had to be incarnated, live a sinless life, die on the cross for your sins, rise again the third day, ascend to the Father, plead for you as your Mediator, and finally come again to gather you home. These are the seven greatest facts worth knowing. If a man knows everything else in the world and doesn't apply these facts to his life, he will miss everything. In the Bible the number seven is the complete or perfect number. So it takes these seven facts about Jesus to make the complete gospel. Every one of these seven provisions is absolutely essential to the true gospel plan. If any of these piers are removed, the bridge will break down. He who denies or fails to accept any of these seven facts is leaving for himself an uncrossable gap in the bridge over the river of sin and death.

Many professed Christians today regard too lightly or attempt to discredit entirely these fundamentals of Christianity. They claim to believe in Christ and yet are actually attempting to undermine these mighty pillars that support the gospel bridge. Some discredit the virgin birth and make void the Incarnation. Others claim that Christ broke the Sabbath and thus discredit His sinless life. Still others reject the idea that Christ died as our Substitute and Surety; they make void the cross and the blood. There are those who claim that His bodily resurrection and ascension are only figments of superstitious imagination and tradition. Many deny the literal return of Christ, making void that last essential section of the bridge that puts us on that better shore. Paul warns us not to listen to any teaching that would call the gospel in question. He wrote to the Galatians, "Though we, or an angel from heaven, preach any other gospel unto you than that which we have preached unto you, let him be accursed" (Galatians 1:8).

Please note that the gospel isn't mere speculation. It isn't theory. It isn't merely theology or philosophy. It isn't subjective truth to be reasoned out by the process of logic. Rather, it is objective truth—real facts about a real person who lived here on earth. Christ was born. He lived sinlessly. He died. He rose bodily. He ascended victoriously. He pleads effectively. He comes again gloriously.

The gospel it just as sure and true as any facts that scientists have discovered by experiment and demonstration in the laboratory. These seven facts constitute an unshakable foundation for an intelligent faith in the life to come. They actually bridge the river of death. We are not left to rest our hope of eternal life beyond this world upon hoary traditions, feasible logic, or appealing philosophy. Christianity is no cunningly devised fable. The gospel consists of facts that furnish a satisfactory basis for infallible assurance that Christ can and does save him that believeth. Well may we sing, "How firm a foundation, ye saints of the Lord, / Is laid for your faith in His excellent word!" and "On Christ, the solid Rock, I stand; / All other ground is sinking sand."

These seven facts have never been true of any person who has ever lived—except Jesus. They will never be true of any other person who ever will live. Hence Jesus will never be surpassed. There will not be and cannot be any new religion that will ever supplant or supersede Christianity. These seven facts make Christianity the only true religion. "Other foundation can no man lay than that is laid, which is Jesus Christ" (1 Corinthians 3:11).

Salvation is simply the making of a personal application of these seven facts to our lives. In order to be saved and cross this great bridge from sin and death to life eternal, we must personally accept these facts. We must say, "Christ was born for me. He lived for me. He died for me. He rose for me. He ascended for me. He pleads for me. He will come again for me."

One of the greatest perils we face in these last days is having a form of godliness without its power. Many are baptized and join the church without receiving Christ as their personal Savior. Many have never personally accepted Christ or received Him. Many have only a secondhand religion.

I appeal to those Christians to whom Christ has not been real, will you not say from your heart, "This day I accept the Lord Jesus as my Savior from sin"?

CHAPTER 11

History and Future Work of Seventh-day Adventists

Uriah Smith

———————◆◆◆———————

Uriah Smith *(1832–1903) became editor of the* Advent Review and Sabbath Herald *when he was twenty-three years old, and, with the exception of a few months here and there, he remained connected with that magazine and the publishing house that printed it until he died. He also served as General Conference treasurer for a year, as the first secretary of the General Conference, and as an instructor in Bible at Battle Creek College. His best-known book is still being sold, now under the title* Daniel and the Revelation. *Smith preached this sermon on Sabbath, October 26, 1889, at the General Conference Session held in Battle Creek, Michigan.*

H e said unto me, Thou must prophesy again before many peoples, and nations, and tongues, and kings" (Revelation 10:11). The theme assigned to me is the history and future work of Seventh-day Adventists. I have taken as my text a passage that I think covers both branches of this subject—a text that, I believe, we have already partially fulfilled.

First, as to the history of this people: previous to the passing of the day that had been set for the Lord to come in the autumn of 1844, there were no Seventh-day Adventists in the world. When I make this declaration, you will understand that I use the term *Seventh-day Adventist* in a restricted sense, applying it to this modern movement that is represented by this congregation here this morning. There has been in ages past no lack of those who have kept the seventh day and who have believed in the personal second advent of Christ; in that sense, they might correctly be called seventh-day adventists. Enoch was one of these; Noah was another; Moses was another; the prophets were others; and so were the apostles. God has had His witnesses all through the ages to these great truths. But these were seventh-day adventists in a more general sense, not in the specific sense in which we use the term as applying to this people who are called out in the last days in a work of reform relative to the interpretation of prophecy and the keeping of the commandments of God.

It was the passing of the time [the Great Disappointment of 1844] that developed this people known as Seventh-day Adventists. That disappointment, so grievous to those who had engaged in that work with sincerity of heart and purpose, threw them back upon the investigation of the Scriptures more carefully to understand why the disappointment had occurred. They were expecting a definite event at a definite time.

Those people reexamined the subject of the time. They found the argument invulnerable: the 2,300 days must end in the autumn of 1844. Then they looked at the event that the prophecy declared should take place at the end of those days. It was that the sanctuary should then be cleansed [Daniel 8:14]. They had supposed that meant the burning of this earth, that its cleansing was to be by fire. So they said at the end of the 2,300 days in 1844, Christ would come. But the days ended, and Christ didn't come. When they reexamined this subject, they found that the cleansing of the sanctuary was not the burning of the earth and the coming of Christ. Rather, it was the entrance of our High Priest into the Most Holy Place of the sanctuary on high, there to perform a work of atonement corresponding to the yearly work of atonement performed by the typical priest in the typical sanctuary here on earth from Moses to Christ. They saw that while they had been correct in the time, they had been looking for the wrong thing.

A new field opened

Having discovered their mistake, a new field was opened before them. They saw that there was a work to be wrought in heaven by our great High Priest before He would come, and that gave time for a further work to be accomplished here upon the earth. They read in a new light the prophecy of Revelation 11:19: "The temple of God was opened in heaven, and there was seen in his temple the ark of his testament." They remembered that the ark was placed only in the Most Holy Place of the sanctuary, and that apartment was opened only when the high priest went in on the tenth day of the seventh month to make an atonement before the ark. Here they saw the same work revealed in heaven. Here was the cleansing of the sanctuary.

They received a new view of the law of God, since its antitypical position in the ark of heaven connected it with its typical service in the sanctuary here on the earth—utterly and forever precluding the idea of any change in that law through all the intervening ages. It must read in the ark in heaven just as it read here in the ark on the earth. Then they remembered that that law said, "The seventh day is the Sabbath of the LORD thy God," and there had been no change in it.

In the same light they read the prophecy of Revelation 14:9–14, where they found a message, equally important in its sphere, to go forth to the world based on what that ark in heaven contains and the ministration that Christ was performing before the ark. So they saw another message—one heralding a reform on the commandments of God and the faith of Jesus—that was to go forth with a loud voice to the people of the earth. They very soon saw that this prophecy related to certain symbols found in Revelation 13. It was a warning against a certain symbol—the two-horned, lamblike beast—which is a symbol of our own government. It was a warning against religious legislation, which, in the light of this prophecy, they saw was to be enacted in this nation—legislation that would compel people to worship contrary to the law of God.

Thus a people were brought out who believed that all the prophetic periods had ended, that we are now in the period of the cleansing of the sanctuary, that the two-horned beast is a symbol of the United States, that a great contest between the commandments of God and the requirements of the man of sin is to be instituted here in our own land, and that the third angel's message, warning against bowing to the man of sin, is now going forth. These are the Seventh-day Adventists of our day. And thus this movement was born.

After the passing of the time, great confusion naturally came into the rank of believers in the Second Advent, and the deportment of not a few of them began assuming very fanatical forms. Wrong views were springing up in almost every quarter, and many were coming to very erroneous conclusions. Out of such a people the first converts to the message of the third angel had to be made because the ears of all those outside the body of Adventists were at that time closed to the investigation of any prophetic themes. Under these circumstances it was necessary that to balance unsettled minds there should come forth some clear, harmonious truth connecting directly with the past and explaining the present situation. And it was necessary that some testimony should be borne, coming to the hearts of men with a higher sanction than mere human reason, to lead the mind forward into that path of a clearer prophetic interpretation that was then opening.

Both these conditions were supplied providentially in the beginning of this work: The first condition was met in the clear exposition of the subject of the sanctuary that explained the mistake that had been made. In connection with the third angel's message, this exposition of the prophecy showed that there had been no failure of any essential feature of the past, and those who had looked forward to Christ's advent had nothing essential to give up. Through their strange experience they had been led forward to an advanced position, into a new light, and the work they were then called upon to do was only a part of the one great work in which they had already been engaged. The other condition was supplied in the spiritual gift, as manifested in the experience of Sister White. That gift rebuked fanaticism, exposed hypocrisy, and detected dishonesty, and it gradually led the minds of honest seekers after light and truth out of that exclusiveness of view, both of belief and of labor, that they were naturally falling into under the impression that their work for the world was done.

"Thou must prophesy again"

Then they began to see the application of the words of the text, "Thou must prophesy again before many peoples, and nations, and tongues, and kings." This was the Voice they now heard speaking to them and opening before them a wide field of labor. But how could they, less than a half dozen strong, take hold of such a work as that? It was an immense work. Would they not have been justified in saying, "Well, it does seem to be true that there is another message to go forth, and the world is to receive another warning. But it will require an immense amount of means to carry forward this work, and it will require a large army of workers to accomplish it. When God raises up the workers and the means, then we will take hold of the work"? But they didn't stop to crucify faith in that way. They knew only that they had been "begotten again to a lively hope" by a new and stirring truth, and they stopped only to know that it was their duty to bring that truth as rapidly as possible to all those whom they thought could be benefited by it. So they took hold of the work of seeking recruits to rally around the advancing standard, and they hailed as a happy victory every accession to their feeble ranks.

To accomplish His work, God chooses earthen vessels and feeble instruments so the glory may be of Him and not of man. It was emphatically so in the beginning of this work. There were no men of means nor moneyed institutions behind it to give it financial strength, and there were no titled names to give it prestige. Those in whose hearts the truths of the third angel's message first took root were persons of very small worldly substance, and that substance had been almost wholly spent in the previous work in which they had been engaged. The little they might gain by daily labor constituted their only financial resources. But their spiritual vision was growing clear, their wills were strong, their hearts were happy and brave, and their courage was invincible. And so, though feeble in health, without friends, and in the face of rising opposition, they began to proclaim that message which they believed was to enlighten and to warn the world. Against the dark background of their circumstances and their condition, their faith stands out in a light that is truly sublime.

The year 1854 was a year of some discouragement in this cause. In the early part of its history, our work had difficulties to contend with that those who have recently come to the faith know very little of. One of the first of these was opposition to all organization and church order. Some of those who embraced the faith had come from other churches from which they had been expelled not on scriptural grounds but by the creed power, for cherishing the blessed hope of the soon-coming of Christ. Consequently, these people had developed such an aversion to all church organization that they were willing to cast the whole aside—the good as well as the bad. But Elder James White saw that there must be some organization, that we must have that unity which comes from a regularly established church membership and church records and church discipline. He saw that organization was necessary to guard against confusion everywhere and to shield ourselves from impositions of every kind.

Those who thought organization all wrong struck against Brother White's initiative, and the cause was threatened with ruin over the question. But those who held the better view calmly urged their reasons till the point was gained and church order was established among us. The same feeling came up to some extent over the adoptions of a denominational name and the incorporation of legal associations—there was at times great agitation over these questions. But at length these difficulties were all happily overcome.

I often think of the time when Elder Loughborough, a few others, and I, under the direction of Brother White, were preparing the first tracts to be sent out to the people. The instruments we had to use were a brad awl, a straightedge, and a penknife. With the awl, Brother Loughborough would perforate the backs for stitching. The sisters would stitch the tracts. And then with the straightedge and penknife, I would trim the rough edges on the top, front, and bottom. We blistered our hands in the operation, and often the tracts were not half so true and square in form as the doctrines they taught.

I often try to imagine what our emotions would have been could we have been suddenly transported to this time, and looked upon these institutions and the wonderful facilities now provided for carrying on the work, and heard the reports we have heard here, and so have been brought face to face with the great advancement that this cause has made. I think we would have felt like exclaiming, "It is enough; now lettest thou thy servant depart in peace." The contrast between that time and this is no less real and striking because it has taken a few years to accomplish, and now we do not feel like departing just yet because there is a future to this work.

What is that work to be?

Our future work

In the scale of nature, we look down below ourselves and find minute forms in comparison with which we are figures of towering size. But when we turn our eyes upward, we see forms and magnitudes so mighty that in comparison with them we are but as the small dust of the balance. So in our work: though it may seem large now as compared with its past, it may take on proportions in the future that will dwarf its present magnitude to very small dimensions. Indeed, it *must* do so if certain prophecies that we apply to it are ever to be fulfilled. We are as yet a small people. We have nothing over which to boast. Of ourselves we can do nothing. And yet there is a mighty work to be done. In the Lord alone is our help, and to Him we look and not to the obstacles that lie in the way.

I read that the third angel's message, which this work embraces, is to ripen the harvest of the earth. Then it must touch wherever there is any harvest to be gathered from the earth. And what does Christ say? "The field is the world," and "the harvest is the end of the world." If this work is to ripen the harvest for the end, it must result in bringing out a perfect church. It must also result, on the other hand, in causing those who fight against it to reach perfection in their line—to go to the extreme of apostasy from righteousness and truth. It is the savor of life unto life, and of death unto death to the last generation. And a work so solemn, close, and searching in its nature will not permit any double minded-ness on the part of its adherents, no division of purpose, no communion with the world, no alliance with sin.

This work is to go forth in the spirit and power of Elias. It will not quail before the Ahabs of this generation. And when the world is writh-ing in the agony of the last great time of trouble as set forth by the prophet Daniel, and when God's people are charged with being the authors of these calamities, as they have been under similar circum-stances in the past, they will boldly answer, It is not we who are trou-bling Israel but ye and your father's house in that ye have forsaken the commandments of the Lord and have followed Baalim.

Our work is to take the front place in one of the greatest controver-sies and the widest scenes of agitation this world has ever seen. In it the long issue between light and darkness, between truth and error, is to reach its climax. It is no less than a decision—not merely an agitation but a final decision—regarding the thrilling question, Shall we follow the Lord Jehovah, or, turning against Him, shall we follow the man of sin? Its principal theater is to be a country that can measure strength politically with any power on the earth, that in resources and wealth overtops them all, that has reached the highest pinnacle of enlighten-ment, that has given to its citizens the sweetest taste of liberty—reli-gious and civil—that man has ever enjoyed.

Here I say will be the principal theater of the controversy, though it will extend to all lands that are influenced by the doctrines inculcated by the "man of sin." Providentially, the lines of the controversy are so laid that in a country like this, before the opposition can carry its points, it must override and break down this boon of religious freedom. Revela-tion 13:12 shows that the two-horned beast—symbol of the United States—is to enact that all shall worship the first beast—symbol of the papacy. That worship involves the right of conscience.

Shall men be compelled to worship against their conscience? Shall church and state be united? Shall religious liberty be overthrown? Shall the principles of our Constitution be trampled under foot? These are the real issues that are coming up in connection with this work. And when the people understand them and see that liberty is imperiled, the controversy will rise to a white heat all over this land. It will divide every state, every county, every city, every village, every neighborhood, every district, every church, and almost every family, and the country will be shaken by such a storm of conflicting views and principles as it has never seen before. Then shall we be called upon to work as we have never worked before. Brethren, the providence of God is drawing us into the very vortex of that great whirl of events with which this world's history is to close. We would do well to begin—and to begin *now*—to strengthen our hearts in Him and gird ourselves for the fray.

The halfhearted and the indifferent will never endure the ordeal. That day will require the faithfulness of the prophets, the love and zeal of the apostles, and the spirit and consecration of the martyrs. Nothing less than this will carry us through. I tremble for those who, careless and indifferent at this time, are content to fritter away their days in trifles and who see no necessity of throwing themselves heart and soul into the work of the Lord and making their connection with Him sure.

Again, Christ said in Matthew 24:14, "This gospel of the kingdom shall be preached in all the world for a witness unto all nations; and then shall the end come." The gospel of the kingdom could not have been brought out in all its fullness until we reached the time and the circumstances of the last closing message. We believe we have it now. This message must go to all the world.

The work of the third angel

We read in Revelation 18:1 that an angel comes down from heaven and the earth is lightened with his glory. This symbolizes, as we believe, the closing of the work of this third angel's message in the earth. The work is certainly worldwide. I dare not venture upon any statistics as to how many papers will have to be published or millions of books circulated, but I think we can safely say that we may every one of us consider ourselves enlisted as soldiers and laborers in this work. The limit of our field is the limit of the world itself.

You ask how long before the work will be done. The outlook is to my mind growing very much restricted. Outside of our own work there are now only two questions to be settled: the Eastern political question, and the Western religious-liberty question. The papacy, as such, has had its day, though as a spiritual power it will live and have an influence till the end. But the great trouble is with a retrograding Protestantism. If Protestants would all stand true to their principles, the papacy would be as helpless as a paralytic. But Protestantism is turning its back upon its own glory. Sometimes a patient partially recovers from a disease but then relapses and dies. Protestantism started out well and partially recovered itself from the disease of papal superstition and corruption. But it has relapsed and is about to die. We see the sad symptoms all around us in the false principles they adopt, the reckless assertions they make, and the bitter and malignant spirit many even now manifest in their movements toward the formation in this country of that prophetic "image of the beast."

How speedily is it possible for that image to be formed? That depends upon public opinion, and public opinion is a fickle thing. It may change in a night. Organizations of immense influence and power are besieging Congress to pass such laws and so amend the Constitution as to virtually unite church and state. Then the image would be here. And who can say that Congress might not take such action at the very next session, and the states by special sessions of their legislatures endorse it, and so we, almost before we know it, find ourselves in the very grip of the coming storm? I say, who knows?

And in the East, all Europe trembles today on the verge of an all devastating war. It would hardly seem possible for this to come without bringing the Turk, the "king of the north," to his end with none to help him. And then, the prophet says, Christ takes His throne and comes as King.

But some may say, You cannot do the work that you admit is to be done in a generation of time. From a human point of view, this might be so. But there is another point of view that takes in Omnipotence. We have One who is mighty to help. I do not blame the twelve spies for reporting that the cities of the Canaanites had walls built up to heaven and that there were giants in the land in comparison with whom they were but as grasshoppers. But I do blame the ten for forgetting that even if the walls were built up to heaven, there is a God *in* the heavens, *higher* than the walls; and though the giants were mighty, the arm of Jehovah was stronger than all of them together, and He was pledged for their help.

So I blame no one now for looking at the magnitude of the work and the seeming difficulties in the way. But I should blame anyone if he forgot that there is a God in heaven who has called for this work to be done and is pledged to help if we will work with Him—a God who could send legions of angels if necessary to the help of His people and who can give to every laborer, every herald of the cross, sinews of steel and a tongue of fire. In God is our help, and to Him alone we look, not to the difficulties of the way and the greatness of the work to be done. In His name and by His help we are well able to go up and possess the goodly land.

The goodly land! I can hardly forbear, before I close, casting a glance forward to that heavenly inheritance that is the objective point of all our struggles, our toils, and our desires. I see there a land that stands in wonderful contrast to this. As the hymn says, "Oh! how unlike the present world, / Will be the one to come!" I see fields smiling in living green, trees majestic in their wealth of verdure, flowers dazzling with their rainbow hues. And on neither field nor tree nor flower do I see the touch of frost or the pale hand of decay.

I see no footprints of the curse, no scars of sin. I see no pestilence walking in darkness nor destruction waiting at noonday. I see no forms distorted with pain nor brows furrowed with anxiety and care. I see no mournful shafts telling where weary forms and sad and broken hearts have gone down into dust and darkness. I see no painful messages passing over that land as two days ago we received here, telling that a friend, a brother, a fellow laborer, had fallen beneath the cruel stroke of a relentless foe. I see no darkened room where the tide of a precious life is ebbing slowly away. I see no bosoms heaving with anguish, no badges of mourning, no funeral trains, no yawning, insatiate grave.

To the contrary, I see a glorious company who bear bright palms of victory over death and the grave. I see, as one of our hymns says, that "the glory of God like a molten sea, / Bathes the immortal company." I see every eye sparkling with the fullness of the joy that reigns within. I see on every cheek the bloom of eternal youth and everlasting health. I see every limb lithe and strong. I see the lame man leaping as an hart. I see the blind gazing with rapture on the celestial glory. I see the deaf listening enchanted to the heavenly melody. I see the dumb joining with loud voice in the anthems of praise. I see the mother clasping to her bosom the children she had lost awhile in the land of the enemy but now recovered forever. I see long-parted friends meeting in eternal reunion.

I see a river so pure and clear, so charged with every element of refreshment and life that it is called "the river of life." I see a tree overarching all so healing in its leaves, so vivifying in its fruits that it is called "the tree of life." I see a great white throne in whose effulgence there is no need of moon or sun to give us light. I hear a Voice saying to that victorious company, "This is your rest forever; and you shall no more be acquainted with grief; for there shall be no more pain, and sorrow and mourning have forever fled away." And in all the universe I see no trace of sin or suffering, but I hear from every world and from every creature a joyous anthem like the sound of many waters going up to God; and they say, Blessing, and honor, and glory, and power, be unto him that sitteth upon the throne and unto the Lamb forever and ever.

Such is the goodly land we may go up and possess. Such is the land that awaits every laborer who is faithful to the end. The Spirit and the Bride say, Come; and whosoever will, may come. If any here have not yet turned their feet Zionward, let me say, "Come with us, and we will do thee good."

CHAPTER 12

The Exodus Movement and the Advent Movement

W. A. Spicer

———◆◆———

William Ambrose Spicer (1865–1952) became the foreign mission secretary of the General Conference in 1892, and the next year helped to establish Solusi Mission in Africa. In 1898 he went to India, where he soon became leader of the church's work in that country. He went on to serve as secretary of the denomination's Mission Board, General Conference secretary, General Conference president (1922–1930), and then field secretary until his retirement in 1940. This piece, which gives one a good feel for Spicer's style, comes from his book Certainties of the Advent Movement.

The deliverance of Israel from Egypt and their march to the land of promise was set as a lesson for all time to come. It illustrates the mighty power of God to deliver. The Christian believer's individual life is a pilgrim journey to the Land of Promise. Every soul knows the bondage of sin and the fettering power of natural habits. Human nature must be delivered from Egyptian bondage,

> For Pharaoh lives in every age,
>   To covet lust and power and might;
> And slaves to serve him are they all
>   Who know not God and shun the right.
> Today—alway—a Shepherd's voice
>   Is lifted up to urge His plea,
> Where wrong enthroned grows hard of heart,
>   And will not let the people free!
>   (Leiser)

Like Israel of old, pilgrims on the way to the better land today must know the delivering power of God. There are Red Seas to cross through which God's providence alone can make the path. He can do it. He who "made the depths of the sea a way" can still make a way where there is no way. We must have His blessing to make sweet the bitter waters of life's Marahs. All through the wilderness journey, thank God, the pilgrim on the way to the promised Canaan may drink like Israel of old from the living waters gushing forth from the riven rock, while the soul is fed with the daily manna fresh from heaven. Of the whole body of believers heavenward bound, it will at last be said as the apostle said of Israel that all passed "through the sea; . . . and did all eat the same spiritual meat; and did all drink the same spiritual drink: for they drank of that spiritual Rock that followed them: and that Rock was Christ" (1 Corinthians 10:1–4).

The Exodus movement became a type of the experiences of each redeemed soul. One old writer, the learned Dr. Lightfoot, says, "The Book of Exodus by the ancient Jews was called the Book of Redemption."[1] But more than merely a type of the experience of the individual believer, the Exodus movement becomes a type of the gathering of the people of God throughout the gospel age and especially of the closing work when the Lord actually gathers a people from all the ends of the earth, making them ready to march together into the eternal Canaan as the Savior comes to lead His people in.

The prophecies foretelling the worldwide gospel work flash out with special light for the last days, when the work is to be brought to a triumphant conclusion. Again and again prophecy of the final deliverance draws its figures and illustrations from the wonderful deliverance when God led His people out of Egypt and on to Canaan.

Dr. J. A. Wylie, the same who wrote the well-known *History of Protestantism,* has written an illuminating paragraph on this feature of the prophecies. He says,

> When the Bible foretells a deliverance from Egypt, and a deliverance from Babylon, in an age yet to come, and paints, as it does, a triumphal procession of escaped captives coming "unto Zion with songs and everlasting joy upon their heads," it is not the literal Babylon that is meant, it is no repetition of the literal drama for which we are to look, but a drama which, while it will greatly transcend the former in its scale, will nevertheless be the same in its essential principles,—will resemble it in the power and goodness of God, and the victory it will bring to the church. We cannot safely ignore, in our interpretations of prophecy, the underlying typology of Providence. . . . On this principle, we firmly look for the providence of God culminating in a grand and universal deliverance of the church. Every one of her former deliverances was a step toward her final deliverance.[2]

It is not until the last gospel work is accomplished and the children of God of all the ages are led into the eternal kingdom that the living

God ceases this work of redemption to which He has set His mighty hand. And the prophecies concerning the last days tell of the special Advent movement proclaiming the message of preparation for the coming of the Lord and gathering out a people prepared to meet Him from "every nation, and kindred, and tongue, and people."

Two great movements compared

Speaking through Jeremiah the prophet, the Lord compares this gathering of His people under the gospel call with the gathering of His people from the land of Egypt. He says, "Behold, the days come, saith the LORD, that it shall no more be said, The LORD liveth, that brought up the children of Israel out of the land of Egypt; but, The LORD liveth, that brought up the children of Israel from the land of the north, and from all the lands" (Jeremiah 16:14, 15).

This doesn't mean that the day was to come when the wonderful works of God in the deliverance from Egypt would be forgotten. That deliverance in the Exodus movement was never to pass from memory. The night of the Passover was to be memorialized throughout the generations of ancient Israel until Christ, the antitypical Passover, should be sacrificed for the children of men. "It is a night to be much observed unto the LORD for bringing them out from the land of Egypt: this is that night of the LORD to be observed of all the children of Israel in their generations" (Exodus 12:42).

At the end of the Exodus journey the Lord opened a passage into the land of promise through the river Jordan even as He had opened the passage out of Egypt through the Red Sea. He instructed that the leaders were to take stones from the dry bed of Jordan with which to build a monument to preserve in the memory of their children this wonderful work of God, "That this may be a sign among you, that when your children ask their fathers in time to come, saying, What mean ye by these stones? Then ye shall answer them, That the waters of Jordan were cut off before the ark of the covenant of the LORD; when it passed over Jordan, the waters of Jordan were cut off; and these stones shall be for a memorial unto the children of Israel for ever" (Joshua 4:6, 7).

The leadership of the living God was manifest in the Exodus movement and was a testimony to His power before all the world. The Lord told Pharaoh why He had so mightily stretched forth His hand in Egypt: "That my name may be declared throughout all the earth" (Exodus 9:16).

The nations had never seen or heard of a work like that. The living God had visited His people. He had delivered them from bondage. By signs and wonders He had led them through the wilderness. He had preserved them, men, women, and children, guiding them by springs of water and bringing forth water in the desert when natural sources failed. By manna rained from heaven He had sustained them. The nations round about, looking on, beheld the people of God marching, marching on to the land of promise. As we learn from the book of Joshua, the word that a living God was with the people had gone before them into the land of Canaan, causing the hearts of warlike tribes to melt within them. The Exodus movement was a wonderful movement, led by the living God.

A greater work in the last days

However, the prophecy of Jeremiah tells of a time to come when a greater work would be wrought: "Behold, the days come, saith the LORD, that it shall no more be said, The LORD liveth, that brought up the children of Israel out of the land of Egypt; but, The LORD liveth, that brought up the children of Israel from the land of the north, and from all the lands" (Jeremiah 16:14, 15).

The living God was to call His people, not out of one land, but from all the lands. The same living God who brought a people out of Egypt and led them to the earthly Canaan is to bring a people out of all the lands of earth and lead them this time into the heavenly Canaan. And this work will be wider in its scope—a worldwide movement—and eternal in its results. So, instead of recounting the marvels wrought in that movement when God brought Israel out of Egypt, men would be talking of another movement in which the living God brings His people from all the lands, preparing them to enter the heavenly Canaan when Christ shall come to lead them in.

Indeed, this deliverance is beyond all comparison with the ancient deliverance from the land of Egypt. As a climax to this final work of God, the Lord Jesus comes in glory and calls forth from their graves the faithful of all past ages, who are raised to immortality to join the last generation of believers in the glad march into the eternal kingdom. God's closing work under the worldwide Advent movement climaxes in the grand event for which all heaven and all humanity have been waiting since Adam lost Paradise.

All through the ages, the gospel message has been gathering out the redeemed of every generation. It was not God's plan that these early believers should go into the heavenly kingdom as their lifework ended. Those who sleep in Jesus are waiting to join the triumphant closing of the gospel work on earth. The apostle says they are to share with the believers of the last generation the glad joy of all together entering the kingdom: "These all, having obtained a good report through faith, received not the promise: God having provided some better thing for us, that they without us should not be made perfect" (Hebrews 11:39, 40).

The saints of God of past generations do not enter the eternal kingdom before those of the last generation. And those of the remnant people of God who are alive in the time when Christ shall come will not precede those who sleep in Jesus. They will all be changed together to immortality and together will enter the glorious Land of Promise. Thus the apostle speaks,

> I would not have you to be ignorant, brethren, concerning them which are asleep, that ye sorrow not, even as others which have no hope. For if we believe that Jesus died and rose again, even so them also which sleep in Jesus will God bring with him. For this we say unto you by the word of the Lord, that we which are alive and remain unto the coming of the Lord shall not prevent [go before] them which are asleep. For the Lord himself shall descend from heaven with a shout, with the voice of the archangel, and with the trump of God: and the dead in Christ shall rise first: then we which are alive and remain shall be caught up together with them in the clouds, to meet the Lord in the air: and so shall we ever be with the Lord. Wherefore comfort one another with these words (1 Thessalonians 4:13–18).

This is the glorious triumph foreshadowed by the prophecy when it says that the days were to come when it would no more be said, the Lord lives who brought up the children of Israel out of the land of

Egypt; but rather, The Lord liveth who has brought up His people from all the lands and—in the glorious climax—from all the generations past, to lead them in triumph into the heavenly Canaan.

The earthly Canaan was a "goodly land." However, it was but a land of this perishable, changing world. Despite all the blessings of God upon it as His people remained faithful, it was a land of sickness and sorrow and death. There was no abiding city there. But this eternal land of promise and prophecy, this heavenly Canaan, is a country of which the Lord says, "The inhabitant shall not say, I am sick: the people that dwell therein shall be forgiven their iniquity" (Isaiah 33:24).

Again the prophecy of old described it: "Behold, I create new heavens and a new earth: and the former shall not be remembered, nor come into mind. . . . And they shall build houses, and inhabit them; and they shall plant vineyards, and eat the fruit of them. They shall not build, and another inhabit; they shall not plant, and another eat: for as the days of a tree are the days of my people, and mine elect shall long enjoy the work of their hands" (Isaiah 65:17, 21, 22).

In almost the last words of Holy Scripture the prophet John tells of the vision given him on Patmos of this new-earth inheritance finally to be the home of the saved:

> And I saw a new heaven and a new earth: for the first heaven and the first earth were passed away; and there was no more sea. And I John saw the holy city, new Jerusalem, coming down from God out of heaven, prepared as a bride adorned for her husband. And I heard a great voice out of heaven saying, Behold, the tabernacle of God is with men, and he will dwell with them, and they shall be his people, and God himself shall be with them, and be their God. And God shall wipe away all tears from their eyes; and there shall be no more death, neither sorrow, nor crying, neither shall there be any more pain: for the former things are passed away. . . .
>
> And the city had no need of the sun, neither of the moon, to shine in it: for the glory of God did lighten it, and the Lamb is the light thereof. And the nations of them which are saved shall walk in the light of it: and the kings of the earth do bring their glory and honour into it. And the gates of it shall not be shut at all by day: for there shall be no night there. And they shall bring

the glory and honour of the nations into it. And there shall in no wise enter into it any thing that defileth, neither whatsoever worketh abomination, or maketh a lie: but they which are written in the Lamb's book of life (Revelation 21:1–4, 23–27).

O, how sweet it will be in that beautiful land,
So free from all sorrow and pain;
With song on our lips and with harps in our hands,
To meet one another again!

A worldwide movement

In the prophecy of Jeremiah 16, the Lord compares the Exodus movement with the great movement that is to gather His people from all the lands in the latter days. This prophecy, as the immediate context shows, covers more than any return of the people of Israel or Judah anciently from the lands of their captivity. That was not the subject of the prophecy. In the nineteenth verse of Jeremiah 16, in which the prophet speaks of this future gathering of the people of God from all the lands, he says that when this gathering takes place, "the Gentiles shall come unto thee from the ends of the earth."

The gathering of Israel in the last days means the gathering of the children of faith from all the nations. He counts the believer, the child of faith, as "an Israelite indeed." The promises concerning the gathering of Israel in the last days are promises of the gathering of the children of God of all nations, not merely of Israel after the flesh. As the Scripture says, these promises of the final triumph are all in Christ Jesus. They are for the Jew after the flesh who believes. They are for believers of all nations. "There is neither Jew nor Greek, there is neither bond nor free, there is neither male nor female: for ye are all one in Christ Jesus. And if ye be Christ's then are ye Abraham's seed, and heirs according to the promise" (Galatians 3:28, 29).

Again the Scripture tells us who comprise Israel as God counts His children: "They are not all Israel, which are of Israel: Neither, because they are the seed of Abraham, are they all children: but, in Isaac shall thy seed be called. That is, They which are the children of the flesh, these are not the children of God: but the children of the promise are counted for the seed" (Romans 9:6–8).

These children of the promise, those who believe the promises of God of all nations and tribes, are the people of whom the prophecy speaks when it says, "Behold, the days come, saith the LORD, that it shall no more be said, The LORD liveth, that brought up the children of Israel out of the land of Egypt; but, The LORD liveth, that brought up the children of Israel from the land of the north, and from all the lands" (Jeremiah 16:14, 15).

And where do we find God's final gathering call to His people of all nations? We find this gathering message in that prophecy of Revelation 14 that foretells the Advent movement. In a worldwide movement the final gospel call is to be carried to men as symbolized by the angel flying in the midst of heaven to "every nation, and kindred, and tongue, and people."

Another scripture contains a prophecy of this gospel work through the centuries that at the last issues in the gathering out of the "remnant," or the church of the last days under the Advent movement: "It shall come to pass in that day, that the Lord shall set his hand again the second time to recover the remnant of his people" (Isaiah 11:11).

Isaiah's chapter covers the gathering call of God through all the generations since Jesus was lifted up on Calvary as the "Ensign for the nations." But this eleventh verse plainly closes with the gathering of the remnant people of God from all lands; for the verse proceeds to mention the great nations of that time, Assyria and Egypt and all, east, west, north, and south. The "remnant" are to come from "the four corners of the earth" (verse 12).

As in Jeremiah, this gathering of the scattered Israel and of dispersed Judah means not Israel after the flesh, but, as the Scripture says, the Israel after the Spirit—the believers of all nations and tongues and peoples. Here again, in speaking of the gathering of the believers of the last generation, the comparison is made with the gathering of the people of God under the Exodus movement. In that movement from Egypt to Canaan, the Lord set His hand the first time to gather out a people, leading them into the land of their inheritance. Now, the "second time," God sets His hand to gather His people—this time from all the lands. And He is to lead them, not into a transitory earthly inheritance, but into the eternal Canaan.

More than one hundred years ago, Dr. Adam Clarke, the Methodist commentator, wrote of this verse: "This part of the chapter contains a prophecy which certainly remains yet to be accomplished."[3]

Fulfilling in our day

In our day it is being accomplished. The gathering call is sounding. The Lord Jehovah is the living God. His work is not completed in the earth until the last sinner willing to receive salvation has been saved unto eternal life.

But the judgment hour is speeding on. From the day when man sinned, it was inevitable that the time of reckoning would come. As the Scripture said, "It is appointed unto men once to die, but after this the judgment." It must come at last; and as the prophecy of Revelation 14 shows, the last message of the everlasting gospel is a special warning to men to prepare for the judgment. That warning message is to be carried to every nation, kindred, tongue, and people. The last—the remnant—church of God is to be gathered out and made ready to meet the test of the judgment and the coming of the Lord.

In a worldwide gospel movement—which we call the Advent movement—that message for the last generation is even now being carried to the world. God has set His hand "the second time"—this time to gather the "remnant" of His people, the true Israel of every nation. They are coming at His call. From land to land and from language to language the message of the prophecy is speeding on its way.

The prophecy of Jeremiah 16 that I have referred to represents the message as calling the children of the Lord out from the remotest parts, gathering them "from every mountain, and from every hill, and out of the holes of the rocks." At a camp meeting in the African interior, I tried out this prophecy of the mountains and hills and holes in the rocks.

It was a scene to move any heart. The crowd that night was seated on the ground under the tall eucalyptus trees at Malamulo, row on row of faces upturned in the dim light of the swinging lamps. They had come from scores of villages in the Nyasaland highlands, upwards of seventeen hundred believers.

"How many of you here tonight has God called out of the mountains?" I asked through the interpreter, James Kalilimba. Hundreds of hands went up in the semidarkness of those straight aisles of eucalyptus trees.

"How many of you has He brought out of the hills?" Again hundreds of hands.

"How many have come out of 'the holes of the rocks' into the light of this message?" Not hundreds this time, but scores of hands went up.

"And it is the literal fact," said one sitting by.

The gathering work is going on before our eyes in all the world. The Lord is gathering His scattered flock. His angels are combing the jungles for them. He has set His hand again the second time and is calling into this Advent movement the remotest peoples—from the mountains and hills, and from the holes in the rocks. He knows every honest heart, even in these heathen lands, and they are coming now at His call.

That night as we filed down from the speaker's stand, a thousand voices were singing,

> All hail the power of Jesus' name,
> Let angels prostrate fall;
> Bring forth the royal diadem
> And crown Him Lord of all.

It would melt any heart, as it did mine, to hear those people of mountain and hill and literally of "the holes of the rocks" singing that last stanza,

> O that with yonder sacred throng,
> We at His feet may fall;
> We'll join the everlasting song,
> And crown Him Lord of all.

As the prophetic descriptions of the closing work of the gospel suggest a comparison between the Exodus movement and this closing Advent movement, even so the New Testament Scriptures emphasize the story of the Exodus movement as bearing a lesson especially for the last days. Speaking of the experiences under the Exodus movement, the apostle Paul said, "Now all these things happened unto them for ensamples: and they are written for our admonition, upon whom the ends of the world are come" (1 Corinthians 10:11).

Like all other Scripture, these things were written for the instruction also of past generations. But in a special sense the story of the Exodus movement conveys a lesson for those who live in the time of the Advent movement. In that ancient movement, God set His hand the first time to deliver a people from bondage and to lead them into the land of Canaan. In these last days the Lord has set His hand the second time, and finally, to gather His people of the last generation, the remnant, from all nations and peoples, and to lead them into the eternal Canaan.

1. J. Lightfoot, *Remains* (n.p., n.d.), 29.
2. J. A. Wylie, *The Great Exodus* (n.p., n.d.), 28.
3. Adam Clarke, *Comment on Isaiah 11* (n.p., n.d.), n.p.

CHAPTER 13

Letter to the Romans

E. J. Waggoner

———◆–◆–◆———

Ellet J. Waggoner (1855–1916) first served as a physician on the staff of Battle Creek Sanitarium. However, his heart was in evangelism, so he gave up the practice of medicine and entered the ministry. Two years after he became assistant editor of Signs of the Times *under his father, J. H. Waggoner, who was the editor, he and A. T. Jones became coeditors of that magazine. At the 1888 General Conference Session held in Minneapolis, Jones and he gave the series of messages on righteousness by faith that shook the church. Waggoner preached this sermon "Bible study" on Sabbath, March 14, 1891, at the General Conference Session held that year in Battle Creek, Michigan. It was the eighth in a series on the book of Romans.*

One motive only should actuate the minds of those who study the Word of God, and that is that they may by this study be drawn nearer to God. He is no respecter of persons. He will give His Holy Spirit to any and to all who ask for it. He is just as willing to make the truths of the Bible plain to one as to another. Peace and light may come into your hearts from what is spoken from the desk, but if you don't know the Word for yourselves, that peace and light won't stay with you.

There is but one true help to the Bible—the Spirit of God. That Spirit spoke the words of the Bible, and it is only by the aid of that Spirit that it can be understood. Any man who will submit himself to the Spirit may understand the Bible for himself. If you get your ideas about Christ and His work from the writings of other men, you get it second hand at best. Draw your light straight from the Bible. Learn the Bible from the Bible itself. When our minds are illuminated by the Holy Spirit, although the Word will appear simple, we will find heights and depths in it that will fill us with amazement. We will spend all eternity studying the plan of salvation, and the longer we study, the more we will find to study.

We will commence this study with the sixth verse of the fifth chapter of Romans: "For when we were yet without strength, in due time Christ died for the ungodly." Mark the words "without strength." Christ was offered on the cross of Calvary at one particular time. But that was not the only time when He availed for the ungodly.

Who are the ungodly? They are those who are "without strength." The human family has been without strength from the Fall, and they are without strength today. When men find themselves without strength, Christ is to be lifted up. He says that He will then draw all men unto

Him. So we can look to Jesus as a crucified and risen Savior today just as much as could the disciples.

We sometimes think that we look back to Christ and that the patriarchs and prophets looked forward to Him. Is it so?

We look up to Christ, and so did they. We look to Christ as a loving Redeemer by our side, and so did they. Said Moses to the children of Israel: "It is not in heaven, that thou shouldst say, who shall go up for us to heaven, and bring it unto us, that we may hear it, and do it? . . . But the word is very nigh unto thee, in thy mouth, and in thy heart, that thou mayest do it." The Word, which was Christ the Redeemer, was nigh unto them; and He is nigh unto us.

They all drank of that spiritual Rock that went with them, and that Rock was Christ. The Israelites didn't need to look forward to Christ. He was nigh unto them. He was the Lamb slain from the foundation of the world. He is and ever has been a present Savior to all who made Him so. He was a present Savior to Abel. "By faith Abel offered a more excellent sacrifice than Cain."

By faith in what? By faith in the Son of God, for there was no one else for him to have faith in. So it was that Enoch walked with Christ by faith. He didn't look to some distant future time for the help of the Redeemer. Christ was to him a present Savior, and they walked along together. So in every age of the world, when men have felt themselves to be without strength, then Christ has been a Savior to them. Notice how plain are the words: "When we were yet without strength, in due time Christ died for the ungodly." Abel was without strength, and Christ died for him. Enoch was without strength, and Christ died for him. Abraham and Sarah were without strength, and Christ died for them. His death was a reality to all of these.

How remarkably powerful was Christ to Abraham! That Christ—the Messiah not yet come and who was to come through Abraham—that very Messiah was so very powerful that faith in Him brought forth the son to Abraham and Sarah in order that He might come through that son. At every period of the earth's history, Christ has been a present Savior to those who were "without strength."

Christ died for sinners

"For scarcely for a righteous man will one die: yet peradventure for a good man some would even dare to die" (Romans 5:7). The word in the original signifying "righteous" is a different word from the one that is rendered "good." The word "righteous" here means a man who is strictly honest and upright but about whom there is nothing peculiarly lovable. Scarcely for such an one will anyone die. But for a "good" man—one who is kind and benevolent, who would give all he had to feed the poor and clothe the naked—for a man of this class some would even dare to die. This is the highest pitch to which human love attains. "Greater love hath no man than this, that a man lay down his life for his friends" (John 15:13).

Now note the love of God: He "commendeth his love toward us, in that, while we were yet sinners, Christ died for us" (Romans 5:8). We too often measure God and His love by ourselves and our love. The Lord through David said, "Thou thoughtest that I was altogether such an one as thyself." The unregenerate heart treats as it is treated and judges God by itself, but God's love is altogether different from human love—He loves His enemies.

How wonderful and how matchless is the love of God, and to how great an extent was that love shown by the death of His dear Son! What had the world done to merit goodness at the hand of God? It had joined hands with the enemies of God. It deserved nothing but punishment. Some say they can't accept Christ because they aren't worthy. People who have been professed Christians for years will deprive themselves of the riches of God's grace because they say, "I am not worthy." That is true. They aren't worthy. None of us are worthy. But God commended His love to us in that while we were yet sinners Christ died for us.

Why did He die? To make us worthy; to make us complete in Him. The trouble with those who say that they aren't worthy is that they don't feel half unworthy enough. If they felt "without strength," then the power of Christ could avail them: the whole secret of justification by faith and life and peace in Christ lies in believing the Bible. It is one thing to say we believe the Bible, and another thing to take every word in it as if God spoke it to us individually.

In 1 Timothy 1:15 Paul says, "This is a faithful saying, and worthy of all acceptation, that Christ Jesus came into the world to save sinners." That is exactly what He came for—to save sinners. "The Son of man is come to seek and to save that which was lost." Oh, that men would realize that they are without strength! When they reach that point, then they can have the strength of Christ. That is the strength that is worth something; it is worth everything.

It is a great thing to believe that Christ died for the ungodly. Sometimes we feel almost so discouraged that the heavens seem like brass over our heads, and everything we do or say seems to come back in our faces as if it were worth nothing, and we think our prayers don't ascend higher than our heads. What will you do at such a time? You must thank God.

"Thank Him for what? I have no blessing. I don't feel that I am His child at all. What will I thank Him for?"

Thank Him that Christ died for the ungodly. If it doesn't mean much to you the first time you repeat the words, repeat them again. Light will soon come in. If you feel that you are one of the ungodly, then the promise is yours that Christ has died for you. You are there before Him on your knees because you are a sinner, so you can have the benefit of His death.

What is the benefit of that death? "Much more then, being now justified by his blood, we shall be saved from wrath through him. For if, when we were enemies, we were reconciled to God by the death of his Son, much more, being reconciled, we shall be saved by his life." Many act and talk as if Christ were dead and irrecoverably dead. Yes, He died; but He rose again and lives forevermore. Christ is not in Joseph's new tomb. We have a risen Savior.

What Christ's death does

What does the death of Christ do for us? It reconciles us to God. It is the death of Christ that brings us to God. He died, the just for the unjust, that He might bring us to God.

Now mark! It is the death of Christ that brings us to God. What is it that keeps us there? It is the life of Christ. We are saved by His life. Hold these words in your minds—"being reconciled, we shall be saved by his life."

Why was the life of Christ given? "God so loved the world, that he gave his only begotten Son, that whosoever believeth in him should not perish, but have everlasting life." Then Christ gave His life that we might have life.

Where is that life? And where can we get it? In John 1:4 we read, "In him was life; and the life was the light of men." He alone has life, and He gives that life to as many as will accept it (see John 17:2). Then Christ has the life, and He is the only one who has it, and He is willing to give it to us.

What is that life? Verse three: "And this is life eternal, that they might know thee the only true God, and Jesus Christ, whom thou hast sent."

Has a person who knows Christ eternal life? That is what the word of God says. John 3:36 says, "He that believeth on the Son hath everlasting life." These are the words of the Lord Jesus Christ.

How do we know that we have this life? This is an important question. "We know that we have passed from death unto life, because we love the brethren. He that loveth not his brother abideth in death. Whosoever hateth his brother is a murderer: and ye know that no murderer hath eternal life abiding in him."

Says one, "We know that we will get eternal life by and by."

Yes, that is true, but it is better than that—we get it now. This is not a mere theory; it is the word of God. Let me illustrate: Here are two men—brothers. To all appearance they are alike, but one is a Christian and the other is not. Now, although there is nothing in the Christian's external appearance to indicate it, he has life that the other has not. He has passed from death—the state in which the other one is—to life. He has something that the other does not have, and that something is eternal life. The words "no murderer hath eternal life abiding in him" would mean nothing if nobody else had eternal life abiding in him either.

First John 5:10 says, "He that believeth on the Son of God hath the witness in himself: he that believeth not God hath made him a liar; because he believeth not the record that God gave of his Son." God cannot lie, so when we say that the words of God are not so, we make liars of ourselves. Now, according to this scripture, we make God a liar if we don't believe the record that God gave of His Son.

What then must we believe in order to clear ourselves of that charge—of not believing this record and thus making God a liar? The next verse explains it: "This is the record, that God hath given to us eternal life, and this life is in his Son."

Some people are afraid that this idea of justification by faith and eternal life will get men away from the commandments. But nobody but the one who is justified by faith—who has Christ's life—keeps the commandments, for God says that we are justified by faith, and if we say we are not, then we make God a liar—we bear false witness against Him, and we break the commandment. In the verse just quoted we are told what we are to believe in order to be cleared from the charge of making God a liar. We are to believe that God has given to us eternal life in Christ. As long as we have the Son of God we have eternal life. By our faith in the word of God we bring Christ into our hearts.

Is He a dead Christ? No; He lives and cannot be separated from His life. When we receive Christ into our hearts, we get life there. He brings life into our hearts when He comes. How thankful we ought to be to God for this.

The power of His resurrection

When Jesus went to Bethany, He said to Martha, "I am the resurrection and the life." We have already read about passing from death unto life. How is that done? Only by a resurrection. In Christ we have a resurrection to a new life. Note the following: Paul prays that he may know Him and the "power of his resurrection." What is the power of that resurrection? In Ephesians 2:4, 5 we read, "God, who is rich in mercy, for his great love wherewith he loved us, even when we were dead in sins, hath quickened us [made us alive] together with Christ, (by grace ye are saved)."

Notice, He hath done this, and He "hath raised us up and made us to sit together in heavenly places in Christ Jesus." We were dead, we are quickened, and we are raised up to sit in heavenly places with Christ Jesus. We must have, and we can have the life of Christ today, for when He comes, He will change our vile bodies by the same power by which He has changed our hearts.

The heart must be changed now. It cannot be changed except by the life of Christ coming in and abiding in it. But when Christ is in the heart, we can live the life of Christ, and then when He comes, the glory will be revealed.

He was Christ when He was here upon earth, although He did not have a retinue of angels and glory visible about Him. He was Christ when He was the Man of Sorrows. The glory was revealed when He ascended. So with us. Christ must dwell in our hearts now, and when He comes and changes these bodies, then the glory will be revealed.

Christ gave His life for us (John 10:10, 11). He gave all there was of Him. What was that? His life. He gave it for our sins (Galatians 1:3, 4). We shall be saved by His life. It is the life of Christ working in us that delivers us from the sins of this present evil world. This is a business transaction. Christ gave His life for our sins. Then to whom did He give His life? To those who had the sins to give in return for it. Have you any sins? If you have, you can exchange them for the life of Christ.

In Hebrews 5:2 we learn that the work of the high priest was to be one of compassion. That is why the men who bore the name of priest when the Savior was here upon the earth were not really priests. They had no compassion. They were wicked, grasping men. One passed by on the other side of the man that had fallen by the wayside, whom the robbers had plundered. Christ had compassion: "In all things it behoved him to be made like unto his brethren, that he might be a merciful and faithful high priest in things pertaining to God, to make reconciliation for the sins of the people."

What is done by the compassion of Christ? Strength is given to us. What benefit is the compassion of Christ to us? He knows the strength we need. He knows what we need, when we need it, and how we need it. So the work of Christ as Priest serves one purpose—to deliver us from sin.

What is the power of Christ's priesthood? He is made Priest "not after the law of a carnal commandment, but after the power of an endless life." That is the power by which Christ delivers you and me from sin this day, and this hour, and every moment that we believe in Him.

Christ was immortal before He came to earth. He was God. What is the essential attribute of divinity? Life.

If Christ was immortal and therefore had life, how could He die?

I don't know. That is a mystery, but I am so glad that One did die for us who had life that nothing could touch and that was successful in resisting the attacks of the enemy. Then so powerful was He that He could lay His life down and take it up again.

No one could take His life

Why was it that no one could take life away from Christ? Because He was sinless. If there ever had been another man on earth who lived without sin, he too could never die. But there never was but the One who trod this earth who was perfectly sinless, and that was Jesus Christ of Nazareth. No one could take life away from Him. The wicked had no power to kill Him. He laid his life down. If He had not chosen to do that, no one ever could have taken His life from Him.

God raised him up, "having loosed the pains of death; because it was not possible that he should be holden of it." It was not possible that death should hold Christ. He had power in His life that defied death. He laid life down and took death upon Himself that He might show His power over death. He defied death. He entered right into the realms of death—the grave—to show that He had power over it. Christ laid down His life, and when the time came for Him to do so, He took it up again.

Why was it that death couldn't hold Him? Because He was sinless. Sin had spent all its force on Him and had not marred Him in the least. It had not made a single blot upon His character. His was a sinless life, and therefore the grave could have no power over Him.

We have that same life when we believe on the Son of God. There is victory in that thought. We can have it by believing on the Son of God. Give your sins to the Lord and take that sinless life in their place. He has given His life for them—why not accept the price that has been paid? You don't want the sins, and the life will be so precious to you. It will fill your heart with joy and gladness. We are reconciled by His blood; now let us be saved by His life.

The life of Christ is divine power. In the time of temptation the victory is won beforehand. When Christ is abiding in us, we are justified by faith and we have His life abiding in us. In that life He gained the victory over all sin, so the victory is ours before the temptation comes. When Satan comes with his temptation, he has no power for we have the life of Christ, and that in us wards him off every time. O, the glory of the thought that there is life in Christ and that we may have it.

The just shall live by faith because Christ lives in them. "I am crucified with Christ: nevertheless I live; yet not I, but Christ liveth in me: and the life which I now live in the flesh, I live by faith of the Son of God, who loved me, and gave himself for me."

Yes, we are crucified with Christ; but is Christ dead? No, He has risen again—and then we also have risen with Him.

But we are in the flesh.

That is true; but in the flesh there may be the divine life that was in Christ when He was in the flesh. We cannot understand these things.

They are the mystery of the gospel. The mystery of Christ manifested in the flesh. Everything that is done for man by Heaven is a mystery.

Once there was a poor woman who was afflicted with an issue of blood. In a dense crowd she touched the hem of the Master's garment. Said Christ, "I perceive that virtue is gone out of me." Now that woman had a real disease, and when she touched the hem of His garment she was really healed of it. What healed her? Real power came out from Jesus and went into her and healed her.

These miracles were written for us. Why were they written? "That ye might believe that Jesus is the Christ, the Son of God; and that believing ye might have life through his name." The same life and power that went out from Christ and healed the body of that woman went out to heal her soul. Jesus is ready and willing to do the same today. We can take that same life into our soul to withstand the temptations of the enemy.

There is only one life that can resist sin and that is a sinless life. And the only sinless life is the life of the Son of God. How many of us have been striving to make ourselves sinless. It has been a losing game. But we can have the life of Christ, and that is a sinless life. Thanks be unto God for this unspeakable gift.

CHAPTER 14

"Whoso Offereth Praise Glorifieth God"

Ellen G. White

———❖—❖———

Ellen Gould (Harmon) White *(1827–1915) was a cofounder of the Seventh-day Adventist Church. She possessed what Adventists believe is the prophetic gift described in the Bible. Her visions commenced within a couple months of the Great Disappointment in October 1844, and she spent the rest of her life communicating, by voice and pen, God's guidance and counsel for the Adventist Church and its individual members. Mrs. White preached this sermon on Sabbath, August 1, 1903, in the chapel at the St. Helena (California) Sanitarium.*

Thus saith the LORD, Keep ye judgment, and do justice: for my salvation is near to come, and my righteousness to be revealed. Blessed is the man that doeth this, and the son of man that layeth hold on it; that keepeth the sabbath from polluting it, and keepeth his hand from doing any evil.

"Neither let the son of the stranger, that hath joined himself to the LORD, speak, saying, The LORD hath utterly separated me from his people: neither let the eunuch say, Behold, I am a dry tree. For thus saith the LORD unto the eunuchs that keep my sabbaths, and choose the things that please me, and take hold of my covenant; Even unto them will I give in mine house and within my walls a place and a name better than of sons and of daughters: I will give them an everlasting name, that shall not be cut off. Also the sons of the stranger, that join themselves to the LORD, to serve him, and to love the name of the LORD, to be his servants, every one that keepeth the sabbath from polluting it, and taketh hold of my covenant; Even them will I bring to my holy mountain, and make them joyful in my house of prayer: their burnt offerings and their sacrifices shall be accepted upon my altar: for mine house shall be called an house of prayer for all people. The LORD God which gathereth the outcasts of Israel saith, Yet will I gather others to him, beside those that are gathered unto him" [Isaiah 56:1–8].

"And taketh hold of My covenant." There is much more in these words than many comprehend at the first reading. When the Lord gave His law to the children of Israel encamped at the foot of Mount Sinai, the people with one accord promised, "All that the LORD hath said we will do, and be obedient." In return for their loyalty, the Lord promised to bring them safely into the promised land and to prosper them above all other nations. "Behold," He declared, "I send an Angel before thee, to keep thee in the way, and to bring thee into the place which I have prepared. . . . If thou shalt indeed obey His voice, and do all that I speak; then I will be an enemy unto thine enemies, and an adversary unto thine adversaries. . . . And ye shall serve the LORD your God, and He shall bless thy bread, and thy water; and I will take sickness away from the midst of thee" [Exodus 23:20–25].

During the forty years of wilderness wandering, the Lord was true to the covenant He had made with His people. Those who were obedient to Him received the promised blessings. And this covenant is still in force. Through obedience we can receive heaven's richest blessings.

Those who claim to be Christ's followers pledge themselves to obedience at the time of their baptism. When they go down into the water, they pledge themselves in the presence of the Father, the Son, and the Holy Ghost that they will henceforth be dead unto the world and its temptations, and that they will arise from the watery grave to walk in newness of life, even a life of obedience to God's requirements.

The apostle Paul, in his letter to the Colossians, reminded them of their baptismal pledge, and wrote: "If ye then be risen with Christ, seek those things which are above, where Christ sitteth on the right hand of God. Set your affection on things above, not on things on the earth. For ye are dead, and your life is hid with Christ in God." How much better it is to seek those things which are above than to seek the things of this world and to form our characters after a worldly similitude!

Walking in Jesus' footsteps

Very often I think of the rich promises given us in the Word in regard to God's keeping power. We are kept by His power. How reasonable, then, it is that we should be careful to walk in the footsteps of Jesus. He says, "I am the Light of the world: he that followeth Me shall not walk in darkness, but shall have the light of life." Of those who walk in this light He declares, "Ye are the light of the world. . . . Let your light so shine before men, that they may see your good works, and glorify your Father which is in heaven."

When we mingle with the world and yield to the attraction of its pleasures and amusements, we think much less of God than we would if we were following Jesus in the path of self-denial which He has marked out for us. Let us keep our minds in right relation to God's promises. Then He will keep us, and we shall see of His salvation.

Many are the promises given us by the Lord for our encouragement. At all times we should be ready to show our appreciation of them by expressing gratitude for them. We should thank the Lord for what He has bestowed on us. Everyone takes His gifts; but how many are there who, from morning till night, think enough of God to thank Him for these favors?

We try to be polite to one another, and we teach our children that when they are in company with others, they are to be pleasant and polite, cheerful and courteous. The Lord desires us to be polite in our association with one another. Shall we act in any other manner when we catch the divine rays of the Sun of Righteousness? When the light of Christ's countenance shines upon us and we receive the riches of His grace, shall we not be polite to God? He has done for us far more than any human being can do. He has bought us with a price—and what a price!

In the councils of heaven before the creation of the world, when it was planned that man should people the earth, there arose the question, What if man should sin as Satan has sinned? Christ answered this question. The infinite Son of God pledged Himself that if man should sin, He would give Himself, His life, as a ransom for the fallen race, taking upon Himself the transgression of humanity. The Innocent would bear the sins of the guilty and stand before God to make intercession in behalf of the transgressor.

Adam fell. Christ has fulfilled His pledge to redeem the lost race. By His sacrifice we are laid under everlasting obligation to God. We are to serve Him with our whole hearts. "Ye are not your own. . . . Ye are bought with a price: therefore glorify God in your body, and in your spirit, which are God's." To this end we will put to tax every power God has given us and strengthen our capabilities to the utmost. The talents God has entrusted to us should be increased by cultivation and use. By faithfully using all our powers to God's glory, we shall be able to fulfill His purpose concerning us.

A talent of great value and one that nearly all possess is the talent of speech. Let us be careful not to misuse it. Let us not be rough or coarse in speech. We are to offend no one, not even little children. Christ says, "Take heed that ye despise not one of these little ones; for I say unto you, that in heaven their angels do always behold the face of My Father which is in heaven." The angels who watch over the children bear to heaven every word, be it cheering or disheartening, that is spoken to the little ones.

God's great gift

Our heavenly Father is in living connection with humanity. If there be one in the universe whom we should respect, it is our Father in heaven, for He "so loved the world, that He gave His only begotten Son, that whosoever believeth in Him should not perish, but have everlasting life."

Some may say, "But we have so many trials and difficulties. How can we avail ourselves of this gift and be overcomers?" [Christ was] "tempted in all points like as we are, yet without sin." Why then should we not determine to fortify ourselves against every influence that Satan may bring to bear against us to hinder the formation of Christlike character? The enemy cannot gain possession of us unless we allow him to. If we are connected with the God of heaven, His protection will be over us. Let us, for Christ's sake, begin now to form characters that He can approve. Let us not put off this work until just before His appearing, when it will be too late for us to begin.

In this world we are given a time of probation, a time in which we can become transformed into the divine likeness. This probation has not been secured for us without an effort. Christ humiliated Himself to the lowest depths in order to redeem us.

Laying aside His heavenly honor and glory, His royal robe and kingly crown, He clothed His divinity with humanity and came to this earth as a little child, here to live from infancy to manhood the life through which human beings must pass.

In return for so infinite a sacrifice, what are we willing to do for Christ? The Father has given to His Son all heaven that we may have every opportunity of overcoming the enemy. To us are granted heaven's richest gifts; but how often we fail to reach up and grasp them by living faith! We would have much more strength to resist temptation if we would exercise greater faith. We should cherish and cultivate the faith that works by love and purifies the soul.

There is a heaven for us to win. For our sake Christ left His riches and glory and became poor that we through His poverty might become rich. Shall we not avail ourselves of this opportunity of becoming rich instead of taking the position that we will have our own way? We shall be under the control of either Christ or Satan, whichever master we voluntarily choose to serve. It seems as if those who [are] unwilling to give their hearts and minds to Jesus choose to place themselves under the control of the prince of darkness; [they] do not exercise their reason in regard to the future. If they continue in their wrong course, the eternity upon which they are entering will not be an eternity of life, but of death.

If we give ourselves to the One who gave His life for us, He will take us into relationship with Himself as His children. His life will be our life. "Come out from among them, and be ye separate, saith the Lord, and touch not the unclean thing; and I will receive you, and will be a Father unto you, and ye shall be My sons and daughters, saith the Lord Almighty" [1 Corinthians 6:17, 18].

We cannot be connected intimately with the things of the world without catching the spirit of worldlings who have no respect for Christ or for heaven. We do not say, Separate yourselves from worldly men and women so completely that you will exert no influence over them. No; but as you associate with them, hold firmly to Christ, and speak of Him often. Introduce Christ to your friends. Tell them that you desire to introduce to them the One who is the Prince of life, the Lord of glory, and that you would be glad to have them become acquainted with Him. Let them know of His invitation to all those who are in perplexity and sorrow. He says, "Come unto Me, all ye that labor and are heavy laden, and I will give you rest."

There are no "ifs" or "ands" about this promise. Rest is assured to all who come. "Take My yoke upon you"—not a binding, galling yoke, but one that will give rest in spirit. "Take My yoke upon you, and learn of Me; for I am meek and lowly in heart: and ye shall find rest unto your souls." In the very act of taking this yoke—the yoke of obedience—comes the rest—the rest that we shall find in our experience. Then we shall realize more fully the truthfulness of the words that follow this invitation: "For My yoke is easy, and My burden is light."

As soon as we submit our will to God's will, our hearts are filled with the fullness of His love. How I long to have men and women understand this! How I long to hold up the One altogether lovely, the Chiefest among ten thousand! How I long to present Him in His greatness and goodness, and then to show what He has endured for us!

He was "wounded for our transgressions, He was bruised for our iniquities: the chastisement of our peace was upon Him; with His stripes we are healed"—healed of our sins.

"I love Jesus"

I love Jesus. I was eleven years old before the light broke into my heart. I had pious parents who in every way tried to acquaint us with our heavenly Father. Every morning and every evening we had family prayer. We sang the praises of God in our household. There were eight children in the family, and every opportunity was improved by our parents to lead us to give our hearts to Jesus. I was not unmindful of the voice of prayer going up daily to God. All those influences were working on my heart, and in my earlier years I had often sought for the peace there is in Christ; but I could not seem to find the freedom I desired. A terrible feeling of sadness and despair rested on my heart. I could not think of anything I had done to cause me to feel sad; but it seemed to me as if I were not good enough ever to enter heaven. It seemed as if such a thing would be altogether too much for me to expect.

The mental anguish I passed through at this time was very great. I believed in an eternally burning hell, and as I thought of the wretched state of the sinner without God, without hope, I was in deep despair. I feared that I should be lost and that I should live throughout eternity suffering a living death. But I learned better than this. I learned that I had a God who was altogether too merciful to perpetuate throughout eternity the lives of the beings whom He had created for His glory but who, instead of accepting the Savior, had died unrepentant, unforgiven, unsaved.

I learned that the wicked shall be consumed as stubble, and that they shall be as ashes under our feet in the new earth; they shall be as if they had not been. There is no eternally burning hell; there are no living bodies suffering eternal torment.

When my mother said to me, "Ellen, the minister says that we have been mistaken; there is no eternal hell," I said to her, "Oh Mother, don't tell anybody; I am afraid that nobody would seek the Lord!"

For a time not one ray of light pierced the dark cloud surrounding me. My sufferings were very great. How precious the Christian's hope seemed to me then! Night after night, while my twin sister was sleeping, I would arise and bow by the bedside before the Lord and plead with

Him for mercy. All the words I had any confidence to utter were, "Lord, have mercy." Such complete hopelessness would seize me that I would fall on my face with an agony of feeling that cannot be described. Like the poor publican, I dared not so much as lift my eyes toward heaven. I became much reduced in flesh. My friends looked upon me as one sinking into a decline.

Finally I had a dream which gave me a faint hope that I might be saved. Soon afterward I attended a prayer meeting, and when others knelt to pray, I bowed with them tremblingly, and after two or three had prayed, I opened my lips in prayer before I was aware of it. The promises of God appeared to me like so many precious pearls that were to be received only by asking for them. As I prayed, the burden and agony of soul that I had so long felt left me, and the blessing of God came upon me like gentle dew, and I gave glory to God for what I felt.

Everything was shut out from me but Jesus and glory, and I knew nothing of what was going on around me. It seemed as if I were at the feet of Jesus and that the light of His countenance was shining upon me in all its brightness.

I remained in this state for some time; and when I realized again what was going on around me, everything appeared glorious and new, as if smiling and praising God. I was then willing to confess Jesus everywhere. I seemed to be shut in with God. Oh, what an effect this vision of Christ's smiling countenance had upon me! The sacrifice that my Redeemer had made to save me from sin and death seemed very great. I could not dwell upon it without weeping. For six months not a cloud passed over my mind. Oh, how I loved Jesus! I love my Savior just as much today as I loved Him then.

Answers to prayers for healing

I have passed through much sadness and suffering. Only about a week ago I feared that I might be a cripple for the remainder of my life. Physical infirmities that I have had for twenty-five years began to trouble me, and I knew not but that I should soon be a helpless cripple. But I kept praying for strength. I prayed, "I will keep my petition before Thee, Thou Lord of heaven, until Thou wilt remove the difficulty." And I am glad to be able to say this morning, to His praise, that He answered my prayer. Dr. Kellogg wrote to me that he had sent by express an appliance for me to use in connection with the electric-light bath, by means of which he hoped I might obtain some relief; but the difficulty is removed.

Not long ago I thought that I was losing my eyesight. I was greatly troubled with pain in my eyes, and for a time had to be extremely careful about using them. Generally I am up early in the morning—sometimes at twelve o'clock, often by two, and seldom later than three. While others are asleep, my pen is tracing on paper the instruction that the Lord gives me for His people. Not infrequently I write, in one day, twenty pages or more of matter for my books. But when my eyes began to fail, I could write only at the cost of suffering severe pain.

I told the Lord all about it. "I must have my eyesight, Lord," I pleaded; "I cannot write without it; and I desire to communicate to the people the light that Thou hast revealed to me." He heard my prayer and graciously restored my eyesight. My eyes are not strong; I use them so constantly that they are weak; but day by day the Lord strengthens them sufficiently for the work of the day, and for this I am grateful. Oh, I thank the Lord with heart and soul and voice!

I love the Lord. Last evening, as we met together in our sitting room for worship, it seemed to me as if the Lord Jesus were in our midst, and my heart went out in love to Him. I love Him because He first loved me. He gave His life for me. Last night I felt as if I wanted everything that hath breath to praise the Lord. It seemed to me that we should have praise seasons and that constantly our hearts should be filled so full with thankfulness to God that they would overflow in words of praise and deeds of love. We should cultivate a spirit of thankfulness.

To the fathers and mothers before me I would say, Educate your children for the future, immortal life. Educate them to see the beauty there is in a life of holiness. Bring them to the foot of the cross. Try to teach them what it means to believe in Jesus—that it is to accept Him as our dearest Friend. Help them to understand that He took upon Himself the nature of humanity in order that He might stand at the head of humanity and become acquainted with all our trials and afflictions. He could have surrounded Himself with angels of glory, but no, He condescended to be made like unto His brethren. He was not born as a prince in this world but was of humble parentage. He understands the trials of the poor. He knows all about the temptations we meet in daily life. We may safely put our trust in Him.

Oh, I am so thankful, so thankful, that we have a Savior who can sympathize with us in everything through which we are called to pass! He loves us with an infinite love. Shall we not so relate ourselves to Him that He can fulfill His purpose concerning us? He desires to cleanse us from sin. As John the Baptist was preaching and baptizing on the banks of the Jordan, he saw Christ coming toward him, and, recognizing Him as the Savior, he cried out, "Behold the Lamb of God, which taketh away the sin of the world!" Shall not we decide to let Christ take away our sin? Is sinning so great a pleasure to us that we will decide to continue to grieve the One whose heart is filled with infinite love for us? Why not cease sinning? We can do this by faith if we lay hold on Christ's promises and say, "In my hand no price I bring; / Simply to Thy cross I cling."

Chiefest among ten thousand

Christ asks for our love. Does He not deserve it? Has not He given us instruction at every step? He says, "Whosoever will come after Me, let him deny himself, and take up his cross, and follow Me." He bore the cross of self-denial and self-sacrifice. He passed over the ground where Adam fell. Our first parents were placed in Eden and surrounded with everything that would lead them to obey God. Christ assumed our fallen nature and was subject to every temptation to which man is subject. Even in His childhood He was often tempted. Through life He remained unyielding to every inducement to commit sin. When in His youth His associates would try to lead Him to do wrong, He would begin to sing some sweet melody, and the first thing they knew they were uniting with Him in singing the song. They caught His spirit, and the enemy was defeated. Ah, my friends, Christ is the Chiefest among ten thousand. Praise the name of the Lord!

We are striving to gain eternal life in the kingdom of glory. We may have it if we will to overcome as Christ overcame. We have in heaven an Advocate who knows our every weakness, and He will answer our prayers for strength to resist the enemy. I used to think that when I prayed for forgiveness of sins, I must have in my heart a feeling that my sins were forgiven before I could know that my prayer had been answered. I do not wait for this feeling anymore. I put my whole heart into my prayer, and then I live this prayer. After asking Christ to do certain things for me, I rise and go to work in an effort to do them. Then the sweet influence of the Spirit of God comes over me with such power at times that I feel as if I must break forth into song, to sing His praises. He is good, and praise belongs unto Him.

Christ is our Great Physician. Many men and women come to this medical institution with the hope of receiving treatment that will prolong their lives. They take considerable pains to come here. Why cannot everyone who comes to the sanitarium for physical help, come to Christ for spiritual help? Why cannot you, my brother, my sister, entertain the hope that if you accept Christ, He will add His blessing to the agencies employed for your restoration to health? Why cannot you have faith to believe that He will cooperate with your efforts to recover, because He wants you to get well? He wants you to have a clear brain, so that you can appreciate eternal realities; He wants you to have healthful sinews and muscles, so that you can glorify His name by using your strength in His service. . . .

You may think that you would be unhappy if you should try to serve Christ; but I testify to you that you would be pleasantly disappointed. When you choose to obey the Lord and become one with Him, you will realize that the light of His countenance is shining upon you and that you will see Him as He is when He comes. He will be in all your thoughts, and your heart will be filled with joy. After instructing His disciples to keep His commandments, He declared, "These things have I spoken unto you, that My joy might remain in you, and that your joy might be full." He takes no pleasure in seeing us miserable, but takes delight in seeing us joyful.

Let us consider these things. They are so simple that we can readily keep them in mind. My brother, my sister, every day lift your heart to God in prayer. Say, "Teach me, lead me, guide me." When affliction comes, and you suffer pain, tell Him that you need Him all the more, and that you cannot let Him go; you must have the assurance of His presence. He knows all about your trials. He, the Second Adam, redeemed us from suffering the results of Adam's disgraceful fall. In every point He overcame the enemy, and through His strength we can win the overcomer's reward, eternal life.

If we should dwell upon these themes, we should hear much more thankfulness rendered to God. Those who realize what He is willing to do for them will praise Him with heart and mind and soul. They will fully surrender themselves to Him in order that He may cooperate with them in the work of perfecting a Christian character.

To the patients who have come here for treatment, I would say, Become acquainted with Christ while you are here. Receive Him as your Savior. Come to His feet, and say, "Lord, if Thou wilt, Thou canst make me whole." We desire to see the Great Physician working in this institution; we do not wish to bar Him out. Commit your cases to Him. He is the Great Medical Missionary. Let us learn of Him, and do His works, that we may glorify Him.

Let us pitch our tent a day's march nearer home. Let us determine to "cleanse ourselves from all filthiness of the flesh and spirit, perfecting holiness in the fear of the Lord." Let us come to the waters of life and freely drink of the health-giving stream. May God help us to strike at the root of the matter. We are liable to be content with mere surface work; but we should never rest at ease until we are joyful in the Lord; and then we shall desire to labor for the conversion of others, that they too may receive what we have received from the Life-Giver.

Christ is the Life-Giver and the Crown-Giver. "To him that overcometh," He promises, "will I grant to sit with Me in My throne, even as I also overcame, and am set down with My Father in His throne." Thank God for such a Savior! Thank Him with heart and soul and voice.

CHAPTER 15

The Throne of Grace

James White

———◆◆◆———

James Springer White (1821–1881) and Ellen Gould Harmon were
married in 1846. Three years later, James began to publish the Present
Truth, *the first publication of the Sabbath-keeping Adventists, who eventu-*
ally formed the Seventh-day Adventist Church. His energy and organiza-
tional and promotional abilities lay behind the formation of many of the
church's primary institutions and indeed of the organizational structure of
the denomination itself. White preached this sermon on Sabbath, March 5,
1870, in Battle Creek, Michigan.

T ext: "Let us therefore come boldly unto the throne of grace, that
we may obtain mercy, and find grace to help in time of need"
(Hebrews 4:16).

It is our privilege to come to a throne of grace. And it is a throne that
sinners may approach with boldness. To find justice? No, to find grace,
to find pardon, to find mercy. Do we go there to obtain our pay for
what we have done? No, indeed. After we have done all that we can do,
we are but unprofitable servants. We are invited to come where we may
find grace, not pay. It is our privilege to find mercy and grace. And we
may find help when we need help, and mercy and grace when we are in
our greatest need. What a privilege!

But how does this chapter of Hebrews open? "Let us therefore fear,
lest, a promise being left us of entering into his rest, any of you should
seem to come short of it." The apostle refers to the children of Israel, who
had the gospel preached to them but didn't profit by it because it wasn't
mixed with faith in them that heard it. They fell because of unbelief.

"Let us therefore fear." Fear is an element of our nature. It is right
that we should have fear. We are safest in times of danger when our
fears are excited. We are even exhorted to have fear.

Fear of what? We shouldn't fear that the Lord won't hear us when
we pray. No, we shouldn't, for we are invited to approach the throne of
grace even with boldness. His ear is always open.

Nor should we fear that the Lord is unable to save. He is able to save
to the uttermost. The experience of our Lord Jesus Christ here in this
world shows the strength of God, and the powers He holds in reserve to
save the children of men who walk before Him with fear.

Christ took upon Himself our nature, lived as our Example, passed
under the power of the temptations of Satan, and obtained the victory

over the powers of darkness. He was mocked in the judgment hall and condemned. The nails were driven through His hands and feet. He died on the cross. He was placed in a new sepulcher, a heavy stone was rolled against the door, and a seal placed upon it. All that men and devils could do was done to make the thing sure, to test the power of God.

But on the morning of the first day of the week, one angel comes down, clothed with power. He rolls away the stone and takes his seat upon it. Another angel enters the sepulcher and unbinds the napkins. Then the Voice is heard bidding the Son of God to come forth, and He rises from the dead, triumphant over death and the powers of the grave. And finally, He is taken up to the throne of God, where He lives ever to be our Intercessor and compassionate Priest. We have in this manifestation of the power of God in the history of Jesus Christ eighteen centuries ago evidence that there is power to save sinners, to save to the uttermost. Then do not fear in this direction.

But let us fear lest a promise being left us of entering into His rest, we should come short of it. We need not fear that there is not in reserve sufficient power to save us. The blood of the divine sacrifice is sufficient, if we will avail ourselves of its merits, to remove all sin from us. Yes, He that could raise His Son from the dead has power in reserve to raise all the blood-washed throng, though they may have passed under the dominion of death. We have no need to fear in this direction.

Nor need we fear that there is any lack of love in heaven for sinners. If God "spared not his own son, but delivered him up for us all, how shall he not with him also freely give us all things?" In other words, after bestowing the greatest gift that Heaven could give, will He withhold the lesser ones? No. In the gift of the Son of God we have a pledge of the unbounded love of God toward sinners. There is no lack of love on the part of our gracious God; therefore, there is no ground for fear in that respect.

The right kind of fear

Yet it is right to fear. There is no sin in fearing in the proper way. Then it is right and a virtue. The wrong kind of fear is classed with crimes. "The fearful, and unbelieving, and the abominable," et cetera, will go into the lake of fire. When we have so many evidences of the power of God and the love of God to save us, to fear that we shall not be saved for want of the love and power of God to save sinners is a damning sin. The fear that cannot trust our great and mighty God and the fear that doubts His love, His care, His power and dares not trust soul, body, property, reputation, and all to His hand will go with the unbelieving and the abominable into the lake of fire. Yet we should fear lest a promise being left us of entering into His rest, any of us should come short of it.

It is right to fear lest we shall fail to do our duty. There is virtue in that kind of fear. It is right to watch ourselves with very jealous care and with great fear lest we offend with our tongue. Oh, that unruly member! Fearless, careless talk! That terrible sin among men! It is like a desolating hail or an uncontrollable fire. We should fear lest our words shall be wrong, lest we have a bad influence over others, lest our words shall have a bad influence over ourselves. Do not let your own ears hear corrupt words, low words, angry words, vain words. Fear lest your own words, sounding in your own ears, corrupt your own heart; and fear lest your words corrupt others.

Oh! How much gossip, and clack, and gabble, and talk there is in the world about little or nothing! There is more hurt done in talking—even among those who profess religion—than in almost anything else. Take the Bible, friends, and fear to violate what God has said in reference to your tongue and talk. Try to live it out.

"Let us," says the apostle, "lay aside every weight, and the sin which doth so easily beset us, and let us run with patience the race that is set before us, looking unto Jesus the author and finisher of our faith." Paul goes right on through the chapter and brings up numerous examples of faith.

I have heard ministers say that one person has one besetting sin and another has another besetting sin. One person has this failing, which is his easily besetting sin; another has that fault, which is his besetting sin. But this is not according to the doctrine set forth here by the apostle. Have you a bad tongue? That is one of the weights to which he refers. It is like a millstone hung around your neck. Have you a bad temper? It is like a blacksmith's anvil hung upon you to impede your progress. Have you an avaricious spirit? That is another weight. And so I might go on. We may have many and different weights. But *the* sin that easily besets all is *unbelief.* Paul makes that clear in Hebrews 11 and 12.

Let us fear lest, a promise being left us of entering into His rest, any of us should seem to come short of it. Let me read on and prove my point: "For unto us was the gospel preached, as well as unto them; but the word preached did not profit them, not being mixed with faith in them that heard it."

You see, they were troubled with unbelief. This was their sin. Now let us fear lest a promise being left us, we should come short of it. And then Paul refers back immediately to the unbelief of the children of Israel as an example.

What then is the fear? What does Paul immediately bring up to illustrate his subject? Why, it is doubting Israel. They fell through unbelief. Let us fear lest unbelief gather around us also and sink us in perdition.

There are those who consider themselves extremely wise, careful, and cautious. When any point comes up, they pride themselves on studying it over very profoundly. And they will say very knowingly, "I do not embrace a point till I have examined it on all sides and studied it well." But are such persons always as profound in wisdom as they imagine they are? and in coming to right conclusions? and making right decisions? No, they are sometimes profound doubters.

Thomas was one of these. He said he wouldn't believe unless he should see in Jesus' hands the prints of the nails, and put his finger into the prints of the nails, and thrust his hand into His side. And what did the Lord say to this very cautious doubter? Did He commend his course? Did He say, "That is right, Thomas. You shouldn't believe as long as you can help it. Wait until you are compelled by evidence to believe"? No! No! He said, "Blessed are they that have not seen, and yet have believed." Let us fear lest a promise being left to us, we, through unbelief, should come short of the promised blessing as did the children of Israel.

Some men say that they will not believe anything till every objection is removed and every point cleared up. But I will believe whenever I see the weight of evidence. Just give me the weight of evidence, and I am there. Judges, justices, and courts have to decide questions upon the weight of evidence, and why not we? I dare not wait till every objection is answered and every difficulty is taken out of the way. It is a fearful thing to stand back mulishly until every possible chance to doubt is removed. Show me the weight of evidence—evidence from the Bible, from experience, from the influence of the Spirit of God— and I think I am always safest on that side. When I take a position like that, which usually involves some self-denial and cross-bearing, I believe I meet the approbation of my Lord. I may expect then to meet the blessing of God sufficiently to see all things clearly.

Fear love of the world

We may fear, dear brethren and friends, lest our love of the world shall overcome us. We may fear that we are not keeping the body under, not controlling the tongue, and keeping the passions in subjection as we should. We may fear in regard to ourselves. We may fear our inability to stand. But never, never should we fear in regard to the ability of the Lord to save us. And while we may cast ourselves, as it were, into the dust, and our cry may be, "Unworthy!" at the same time we may sing, "Worthy, worthy is the Lamb." While our confidence in ourselves is growing weaker and we are seeing that we are dependent upon God for everything, our confidence in the Lord may grow stronger and stronger every day.

The devil is always ready to take advantage of our very best qualifications and efforts and use them to his own ends. Take, for instance, the accomplishment of singing. What a blessing is talent and voice and taste for singing! And how, with a sanctified use of it, you may glorify God! But the devil has almost entire control of nearly every good singer. There are more souls sung to hell than are prayed to heaven.

So with fear. It is right to have the proper kind of fear. It is a virtue. But unless you are careful, the devil will come right in and work upon your conscientiousness to drive you to doubts, and to darkness, and to despair. There is no reason for this. You have a sufficient pledge in the power of God in raising Jesus Christ from the dead that God is able to save you. You have a pledge of His love in that He condescended to give Christ to die for you. Under these circumstances it is sin to throw away your shield of faith and to doubt.

"Let us fear," says Paul. But to help the feebleminded ones and lest you should sink in despair, the apostle states in this very chapter, "Seeing then that we have a great high priest, that is passed into the heavens, Jesus, the Son of God, let us hold fast our profession." Hundreds and thousands of Christians have suffered the devil to throw this fear and trembling over them—to pervert this wholesome quality of proper fear that all should have and so drive them into doubt and despair and into laying down their profession. Just hear them talk out their cruel doubts:

"I am so unworthy and have so little faith that it is no use for me to pray any more. I cannot bear my testimony in meeting, and it is of no use to make any further efforts."

But listen to the apostle: "Seeing then that we have a great high priest, that is passed into the heavens, Jesus the son of God, let us *hold fast* our profession." Don't let the devil drive you to despair. We have a great High Priest who can be touched with the feeling of our infirmities. He was in all points tempted like as we are, yet without sin. He is willing and mighty to save. Trembling, desponding ones, look up! Do you say that you are all unworthiness? I respond, Amen! You are. You may just as well set that down for a fact. But Jesus is worthy. He is able. He is willing and ready to save. Then look up, look up. He is your Mediator. He is your Intercessor with the Father. He has been touched with the feeling of all your infirmities, and woes, and sorrows, and weaknesses, and He knows just how to help you.

You have, it is true, sinned against God. You may be an unpardoned sinner in His sight. But think what a glorious link still unites you to that God of justice whom you have offended. Jesus, who has been touched with the feeling of your woes, is your Advocate. And of all the beings in the universe, no one has the influence—to use a common term—with the God of heaven that His obedient, victorious Son has. It is the dearly beloved Son who links you to the Great Lawgiver, and He is your best friend. He loved you so well as to die for you. He has tasted all your woes. He knows all about you. And it is He whom the Father loves; and the pleading of that Son will move the arm of the Father.

He is mighty. We will love Him. With one arm He has hold of the Father, and with the other He reaches down to poor sinners. Under these circumstances you should not tremble and doubt and fear to trust in His grace. No, never.

With such facts before us, it is a sin to doubt. There is all the reason in the world why we should believe. "For we have not an high priest which cannot be touched with the feeling of our infirmities; but was in all points tempted like as we are, yet without sin."

The condescension of the Son of God

What condescension on the part of the divine Son of God to come down and take our nature so He could enter into all our woes, weaknesses, and sorrows! Just think how the devil takes Him up to the pinnacle of the temple. Sometimes we climb onto some earthly pinnacle. Not as our Lord, for the devil carried Him there. We become exalted and lifted up with pride.

See the Lord there while the devil presents before Him all the kingdoms of the world and says, Just fall down and worship me and all shall be yours. Christ resisted this temptation of the gift of all the world. How many men are willing to sell themselves to the devil for but a little gain!

That Jesus might be a merciful High Priest as He undertakes to cure the terrible malady of sin, He is carried into the wilderness and fasts forty days. And as He hungered, the devil brought the temptation of appetite to bear upon Him. The devil caused the representatives of the race to fall on appetite. By this means He has held control over almost all the race ever since.

Look at that drunkard, bound to his cups, a slave of appetite. So with the tea-drinker, the tobacco-user, the glutton. They are slaves to appetite. The world is given up to appetite. If the popular churches of the day wish to raise money for any purpose, they do it through the indulgence of the appetite. A strawberry festival, an ice-cream entertainment, an oyster supper, or something of the kind is the means by which the liberalities of the people are drawn out.

But our Lord was carried into the wilderness in order to be prepared to cure the maladies of our fallen nature. He fasted forty days and He overcame. Oh! My dear friends, there is something in this subject that seems to carry me out of myself entirely as I view it in its importance. What reasons there are for us to watch ourselves with jealous fear, and what reasons there are to have confidence in God!

But, says one, I have sinned and transgressed and pierced His wounds afresh. How can I have confidence?

We reply, He came to save just such as you are. "Then came Peter to him and said, Lord, how often shall my brother sin against me, and I forgive him? Till seven times? Jesus saith unto him, I say not unto thee, Until seven times; but, Until seventy times seven." I do not know why the Lord would not forgive the truly repenting soul as often as He would have us forgive the erring. So, don't be discouraged though you have tried and failed, and again, and again, and failed every time. When you have fallen seventy times seven times, then we may have to give you up as a hopeless case.

Jesus came to save sinners; that is why He took such an infinite stoop. That is His mission. That is His work. The Lord, who never sinned, takes the soul all polluted, all covered with sin, and purifies and exalts and makes it clean. This is His glory. If there is a person who is a greater sinner than others, my word of comfort to you is to come and let Jesus wash you from all your sins and fit you for heaven.

The conclusion from all this is found in the words of the text: "Let us therefore come boldly unto the throne of grace." You need not come fearing and trembling. In the name of Jesus you may come boldly. Those whom He forgives most He loves most. Those who have been the greatest sinners and come along with repentance will find pardon proportionate to their sins. The blessings will be proportionate to the wrongs committed. Are you a great sinner? Then a great repentance is called for, and then a great pardon and a great blessing will be bestowed.

Let us come boldly unto the throne of grace. We must not come carelessly, not pompously, no presumptuously. People sometimes pray as though God were greatly indebted to them, as though they had done a great deal for the Lord: "Lord, bless me; I have done so much for Thee." This is not a holy boldness. Holy boldness is all in consequence of the character of our Mediator. There is not one reason in yourselves why you should have asked Him to forgive your sins—the reasons are all in Jesus Christ. You have a High Priest who can be touched with the feeling of all your infirmities. That is why you may approach the throne of grace with boldness. Have you sinned? Come boldly to the throne of grace that you may obtain mercy and find grace to help in time of need.

Grace to help in time of need! There are a great many professors of religion, who, when they are not in special need, when they do not feel that they have especial wants, will grow careless about offering up their petitions to God for help. But when they are brought into straitened places, into states of anxiety and distress, then they will pray. I might illustrate this by what I witnessed on a steamer on my way from Portland, Maine, to Boston, Massachusetts. A storm was rising, and the sea was rough.

I remarked to the captain that it was getting rather rough. "Yes," said he, "but we still try to iron it down"—a sailor phrase to quiet the fears of the passengers. But he knew there was danger.

I went down to see how Mrs. White was getting along. I remarked upon the roughness of the sea. "Yes," said she, "but God will protect us."

Pretty soon the chandelier came down with a crash, causing a shriek through the whole crowd. By and by the furniture began to tumble about, and the steward began to hold on to the dishes to keep them from being dashed in pieces.

Previous to this time, we had noticed a very wild, rough girl on board. She had been light and reckless in her talk. As the storm increased, she began to cry for mercy. She went to my wife and asked her if she was not afraid. "No," said my wife, "if my work is done, I would just as soon go to the bottom here as any way. But I have no fears; I don't believe my work is done." And so the frightened girl went from one to another expressing her fears and wringing her hands in great distress.

The next morning the storm abated. When we reached the harbor, she was as light and thoughtless and frivolous as ever. And as she sprang to land, she exclaimed, "There, glory to God, I am safe now." This she said in trifling mockery of her own fears.

This may be an extreme case, but it illustrates a general rule. People will not pray till there is danger; and when the danger is over, they are as thoughtless as ever. This is a wrong rule. Let us go to find grace for a time of need. You may need special grace a week from now. Don't put off praying for grace till that time comes; pray for it now. Let your prayers go up even if you don't need special endowments of grace just at this time. Send every prayer into heaven that you can, and depend upon it that when the trying hour comes the needed help will come.

I don't know that in all my experience I ever witnessed anything that affords a better illustration of my views than the following incident. Brother Andrews and I went from General Conference to Greenville very feeble and discouraged. We asked each other, "What shall be done for the cause?" and we walked from wood to wood and from place to place meditating and deliberating upon this question, and praying for strength and help. I was very feeble, many a time having barely the physical strength to support myself.

Eventually, we decided to attend the Wright camp meeting. I came to Battle Creek, then spent one Sabbath at Monterey, and so on to the camp meeting. There we witnessed the especial blessing and power of

God—such power as I hardly ever witnessed in my life. God was then answering our prayers that we had put up to Him weeks before. The answer came just when we needed it. Let us therefore come boldly to the throne of grace that we may obtain mercy and find grace to help in time of need.

"Why," says one, "I have been praying for God's blessing now for a week, and He has not answered one of my prayers."

How do you know but that He has accepted all those prayers and in due time the blessing will come just when you most need it?

The kingdom of grace

"Let us therefore come boldly unto the throne of grace." A throne supposes a kingdom; then is there not a kingdom of grace? My mind is settling here. If there is a throne of grace, there is a kingdom of grace. I lament that Adventists have labored so hard, so tenaciously, to maintain the idea that Scripture, when speaking of the kingdom of God and kingdom of heaven, always refers to the future kingdom of God. It has given our opponents an advantage they have no business holding.

I certainly am looking for a future everlasting kingdom of God—the fifth kingdom, to be set up after all earthly kingdoms shall be destroyed, when the New Jerusalem, the metropolis of the fifth kingdom, shall come down from God out of heaven and the kingdom and dominion under the whole heaven shall be given to the saints of the Most High. When you pray, "Thy kingdom come," you are praying for that kingdom. And when James says, "Hath not God chosen the poor of this world . . . heirs of the kingdom," he refers to that kingdom. "Then shall the righteous shine forth in the kingdom of their Father."

However, there are two kingdoms to which the expressions "kingdom of God" and "kingdom of heaven" apply. These two I shall call, respectively, the kingdom of grace and the kingdom of glory. The kingdom of grace exists now. The kingdom of glory is future.

By no means do I take the position that the kingdom of grace was set up at the first advent of Christ. In no sense whatsoever was the kingdom set up then. Instead, I carry it back to the time when grace was first offered to sinful man. Adam and Abel were in the kingdom of grace as fully as were the apostles. Daniel could approach the throne of grace as well as we today.

In the first chapter of Colossians, Paul says,

> For this cause we also, since the day we heard it, do not cease
> to pray for you, and to desire that ye might be filled with the
> knowledge of his will in all wisdom and spiritual understanding
> [Oh, that we were there today!]; that ye might walk worthy of
> the Lord, unto all pleasing, be fruitful in every good work [Oh,
> that there were with us an undying desire to be fruitful in every
> good work!], and increasing in the knowledge of God; strength-
> ened with all might according to his glorious power, unto all
> patience and long-suffering with joyfulness; giving thanks unto
> the Father which hath made us meet to be partakers of the in-
> heritance of the saints in light; who hath delivered us from the
> power of darkness, and hath translated us into the kingdom of
> his dear Son (verses 9–13).

Here is an expression that I believe applies to Christian experience.
Here is a deliverance from the powers of darkness. This has nothing to
do with the resurrection of the dead. It is a deliverance that every Christian may realize here. This deliverance is a part of their Christian experience.

"Being translated into the kingdom of his dear Son." Here is a work,
too, of Christian experience—to be translated into the kingdom of
grace. Many are under the powers of darkness, yielding to the powers of
an unsanctified heart. We may be delivered from all this and translated
into the kingdom of His dear Son.

Paul continues, "In whom we have redemption."

There, says one, that is future.

Are you sure of it? There are two redemptions: one from sin or a
moral redemption, and then there is a physical redemption from the
dead by the resurrection. But here Paul speaks of redemption from
sin: "In whom we have redemption through his blood, *even the forgiveness of sin.*" That is enough. It all terminates in the complete forgiveness of sins. And John, then, upon the Isle of Patmos, could say,
"I am your brother and companion in tribulation, and in the kingdom
and patience of Jesus Christ." He was there in exile, as a criminal, for
doing right. His banishment only removed him a little nearer God. In
tribulation? Yes. But also in the kingdom—receiving the blessings of

the kingdom of grace in the highest sense while there on the Isle of Patmos.

This theme is glorious, but I will not introduce more testimony now. Let me exhort you to seek for that fullness, that richness of experience that is represented here by Paul to the Colossians when he speaks of our being "filled with the knowledge of his will in all wisdom and spiritual understanding; . . . unto all pleasing, being fruitful in every good work." Amen.

If you've enjoyed this volume, you'll want to read these books as well.

We Have This Hope
Timeless Adventist Sermons, volume 2

"We have nothing to fear for the future, except as we shall forget the way the Lord has led us and His teaching in our past history."
—Ellen G. White, *Life Sketches*, p. 196.

Seventh-day Adventists have long been a "people of the Word." Bible study and fervent preaching have influenced who we are and what we believe. In each generation, God has used dedicated men and women among us to guide and encourage the church as well as to grapple with ongoing discussions of doctrine and mission.

Volume two of *We Have This Hope* presents sermons from the next generation of Adventist leaders. The great preachers of this era include the following: Arthur S. Maxwell, Dick Barron, Glenn Coon, H. M. S. Richards Sr., Fordyce Detamore, Betty Holbrook, and others.

Hardcover, 192 pages. ISBN 10: 0-8163-2279-1.

From Sundown to Sundown
May-Ellen Netten Colón

At the heart of the Sabbath stands a Person—Jesus, our Source of joy.

If you're looking for a recipe for Sabbath keeping with all of the dos and don'ts, you will be disappointed. This book goes beyond the "rules" to the principles of Sabbath keeping and beyond the principles to the *Person* who gave us the Sabbath.

The Bible does not say, "Remember the Sabbath day to keep it gloomy." Need some help in revitalizing your Sabbaths? This is the book for you.

Paperback, 256 pages. ISBN 10: 0-8163-2261-9.

3 Ways to Order:
1. Local Adventist Book Center®
2. Call 1-800-765-6955
3. Shop AdventistBookCenter.com